MY ANCE
WER
BAPTISTS

HOW CAN I FIND OUT MORE ABOUT THEM?

GEOFFREY R. BREED

Published by
Society of Genealogists
14 Charterhouse Buildings
Goswell Road
London EC1M 7BA

First Published 1986
Revised 1988
Third Edition 1995

British Library Cataloguing
in Publication Data.
A catalogue record for this book is
available from the British Library

ISBN 0 946789 84 3

The Reverend Geoffrey Ralph Breed was educated at the City of London School and Edinburgh University, where he read Science. After service as an Army Officer he had a successful career in commerce, later studying Theology at Christ Church College, Canterbury and entering the Baptist ministry. A Baptist historian, his postgraduate studies included an M.A. in history at Keele University.

The cover illustration is from the first Minute of Stroud Baptist Church, Gloucestershire, and is reproduced by kind permision of the Church.

CONTENTS

CONTENTS

PREFACE TO THE THIRD EDITION

Whereas the text has been up-dated and slightly enlarged, the Appendices have been entirely re-written. In previous editions the list of registers at the Public Record Office (Class RG 4) has been extracted from the 1859 publication of HM Stationery Office, *Lists of Non-Parochial Registers and Records in the Custody of the Registrar-General of Births, Deaths and Marriages*, and the PRO references added in. In that publication the span of years covered by each register had been calculated from the dates of the first and last entries contained in it. A continuing project by the PRO to examine every single register, to ascertain the actual starting and finishing dates of each, has now been completed, and this corrected information has been included in this Third Edition. Some registers which were not surrendered to the State in the late 1830s, as required, have subsequently been deposited with the PRO, who have classed them as 'RG 8 - Unauthenticated Registers'. These, too, have all been included in this current listing.

The registers held in Class RG 4 at the Public Record Office are included in the International Genealogical Index (IGI) compiled by the Genealogical Society of Utah. They are arranged by English counties, then alphabetically by surname, then by forename, then chronologically.

Further records have been deposited with the Society of Genealogists, whose Librarian has written Appendix 2, the Gospel Standard Baptist Library, and that of the Strict Baptist Historical Society, and so these Appendices have been re-written to reflect their current holdings.

It is this author's hope that this edition may prove of even greater usefulness to researchers world-wide than its predecessors.

MY ANCESTORS WERE BAPTISTS

The purpose of this booklet is to enable a would-be researcher to gain biographical information concerning Baptist ancestors.

An enquiry is more likely to be successful if some preparatory work is done, and time spent in studying the contemporaneous religious and social climate can provide the background information which makes a biography so much more than an accumulation of statistics.

Before proceeding, some basic facts need to be learned. The Baptist denomination is not a 'church' in the sense that there is a Methodist Church or a Church of England. Both of these churches are centrally organised, each local church being accountable to a denominational headquarters which can provide a systemised record of their ministers and the local churches.

Each local Baptist church, by contrast, is a separate, autonomous body, self-governed by the 'church meeting', which is the decision-making body. Although there are area Associations and a Union of Baptist churches, individual churches can decide whether to join them or remain independent.

Differences in theological emphasis have also been an important factor in Baptist organisation. A brief historical outline is given in each issue of the *Baptist Union Directory* since 1973 and this currently reads:

Organised Baptist life in England had two distinct beginnings. In 1611 Thomas Helwys led back from Amsterdam a small group who a few years earlier had sought religious freedom in Holland and who had there formed themselves into a Separatist church - under the leadership of John Smyth - practising believers' baptism. Helwys was the author of *The Mistery of Iniquity* the first English printed book to plead for full religious freedom. The successors of Helwys and his friends became known as General Baptists. They were Arminian in theology but their church order was previously independent but modified by the appointment of intercongregational officials known as 'Messengers'.

In 1633 a group connected with a Calvinistic Separatist church in London broke away on adopting believers' baptism. This was the origin of the Particular Baptists. They remained Calvinistic in theology but their church order was of the more 'independent' type. The first Baptist church in Wales was founded in 1649 at Ilston, near Swansea. Baptists had founded work in Ireland by the mid-seventeenth century and in Scotland by the mid-eighteenth century. A 'New Connexion' of the more

1

evangelical General Baptists was formed in 1770 under the influence of the Methodist revival by Dan Taylor; certain General Baptist churches remained aloof, however, and of these the majority became Unitarian. The late eighteenth century also witnessed a resurgence of evangelistic zeal amongst the Particular Baptists, as a result of the influence of Andrew Fuller (1754-1815) and others whose Calvinism was actively evangelical in spirit. The formation of the Baptist Missionary Society in 1792, whose first missionary William Carey went to India in 1793, was the most notable fruit of this renewal of Particular Baptist life. The influence of the BMS led in its turn to the formation in 1812-13 of the first Baptist Union amongst Particular Baptist churches. The Union had an uncertain early history, but after its re-formation in 1831-32, Particular Baptists and General Baptists of the New Connexion began to draw more closely together. This process culminated in 1891, when the General Baptists of the New Connexion, under the leadership of John Clifford (1836-1923) amalgamated with the Baptist Union.

Certain churches have remained more strictly Calvinistic, and in general have refused to receive any at the Lord's Table who have not been immersed as believers. They are known as Strict Baptists, usually, and have three regional Associations of Strict Baptist Churches. The Strict Baptist Assembly continued until 1976 when they joined the Assembly of baptised churches holding the Calvinistic doctrine of Sovereign Grace to form the Grace Baptist Assembly.

The Baptist denomination has, over the years, spread to many lands and is today one of the largest Protestant communions in the world, linked in the fellowship of the Baptist World Alliance, formed in 1905.

From this one can readily understand that there is a variety of Baptist organisation and it is necessary to discover to which emphasis the desired ancestor subscribed!

Today, many churches belong to the Baptist Union of Great Britain, but some belong to the various strands of Strict Baptist polity, more usefully classified by the name of the religious periodical whose basis of belief finds the accord of the membership, thus: Gospel Standard (1835 to date); Gospel Herald (1833-1969); Earthen Vessel (1845-1886); Christian's Pathway (1896-1969); Grace (1970 to date). Yet others are completely autonomous, not associated with any other church, association or grouping.

Other Baptist groupings include the Seventh-Day Baptists, whose Sabbath is observed on Saturday. Never great in numbers in this country, they are still of some importance in the United States of America.

The Scotch Baptists who began in the eighteenth century, had some influence south of the border also, and some Baptist churches in England derive from them.

Of more recent origin, the Old Baptist Union which derives from the United States, began in this country in 1880 and currently numbers about thirteen churches.

The Churches of Christ, sometimes known as the Disciples of Christ, are so similar to Baptists in their belief and practice that, in the past, some of their churches have joined Baptist Associations. Nevertheless they have remained separate until quite recently when most joined the United Reformed Church.

Although the majority of Baptist churches in this country are associated with the Baptist Union, the churches retain their autonomy and may choose to send or withhold such statistical and other information which the Union seeks to enable it to compile the annual *Handbook* (now named the *Baptist Union Directory*).

The minister of each Baptist church is chosen by the members of that church, and the title 'Baptist minister' does not automatically carry with it any guarantee of theological training, doctrinal orthodoxy, ordination or accreditation. It simply denotes one who at some time is, or has been, in pastoral charge.

There are some basic introductory works of Baptist history which would well repay study before one launches upon an enquiry about a specific individual. The principal works issued in this century are:

Whitley, W T,	*A History of British Baptists* (London 1st edn. 1923, 2nd revised edn. 1932)
Underwood, A C,	*A History of the English Baptists* (London, 1947)
McBeth, H L,	*The Baptist Heritage* (Nashville, Tennessee, U.S.A., 1987)
Payne, E A,	*The Baptist Union: a Short History* (London, 1959)
White, B R,	*The English Baptists of the Seventeenth Century* (London, 1983)
Brown, R,	*The English Baptists of the Eighteenth Century* (London, 1986)

Briggs, J H Y,	The English Baptists of the Nineteenth Century (London, 1994)
Bassett, T M,	The Welsh Baptists (Swansea, 1977)
Yuille, G,	History of the Baptists in Scotland (Glasgow, 1926)
Bebbington, D W, (ed.)	The Baptists in Scotland (Glasgow, 1988)

From previous centuries, the following two works contain a wealth of biographical information as well as individual Baptist church histories:

| Crosby, T, | The History of the English Baptists [to 1714] (4 vols., London, 1738-1740) |
| Ivimey, J, | A History of the English Baptists (4 vols., London, 1811-30) |

From 1 July 1837 the law has required the registration of all births, marriages and deaths in England and Wales and these records are in the custody of the Registrar-General, who will issue certificates of these events. The current cost [1994] is £5.50 to callers, or £15 by post for each certificate. The indexes alone may be searched by callers free of charge. These are records of separate events and are not linked together in families. Any correspondence about these records should be addressed to the Registrar-General, St Catherine's House, 10 Kingsway, London WC2B 6JP.

In Scotland, civil registration began in 1855, and these records are in the custody of the Registrar-General, New Register House, Princes Street, Edinburgh EH1 3YT, who will issue certificates of these events. Whilst callers need to pay a search fee, this provides access not only to the indexes, but also to a sight of the actual entry. Postal application is also possible, but it would be wise to write initially, as the search fees are not the same as those charged in London for English and Welsh certificates. New Register House is also the repository for many older records of genealogical interest.

In England and Wales before 1 July 1837, the principal means of recording births, christenings (= infant baptisms), marriages and deaths or burials were parish registers kept by clergymen of the Church of England. The best way to trace them is to contact the appropriate county archivist or the minister of the church in which the ceremony is thought to have taken place.

4

BIRTHS

Births of children to Baptist parents were not automatically recorded in the parish registers. This is because Church of England parish registers relate to infant baptisms, a practice conscientiously disfavoured by Baptists. There might anyway be a considerable interval between birth and baptism. Nevertheless, an extract from such a register, termed a 'certificate of baptism' was accepted by the courts as a valid legal document, whereas Nonconformist records were usually not.

However, where the persons were of such status as to need to protect property rights, the occasional services of the Church of England were often resorted to, for security reasons, without too much hurt of conscience. One needs to remember that before the introduction of civil registration in 1837, there was an atmosphere of occasional conformity and it is difficult sometimes to divide what people were willing to do for the sake of the law from what they did out of choice.

Early legislation in 1695 and 1700 to combat this injustice required Dissenters' births to be reported to the incumbent either to be added to his register, or entered in a separate book. Unfortunately these laws were not universally effective, although it does explain the use of the word 'born' against some entries in baptismal registers, usually, but not exclusively, those of Nonconformists.

In other words, the parish register is the first place to look when seeking evidence of any Baptist birth which occurred before July 1837, the more especially because sometimes people changed their religious allegiance. The fact that a person was a Baptist later in life does not necessarily mean that was their confession at the time of marriage, or that they were born into a Baptist family.

Nevertheless, quite independently of parish records, Baptists quite often kept their own church's record of births, marriages and deaths. Not all churches kept records, and by no means have all survived.

Following the 1837 introduction of civil registration, the law required all these Nonconformist registers to be surrendered to the Registrar-General who was then empowered to issue from them certificates which would have the force of law. More recently these 'non-parochial registers' as they are called, passed into the custody of the Public Record Office, Chancery Lane, London WC2A 1LR, where they are classified 'RG 4'.

Although the greatest concentration of surviving non-parochial registers is to be found at the Public Record Office, and these are all listed in a catalogue which was published by Her Majesty's Stationery Office in 1859 under the title *Lists of Non-Parochial Registers and Records in the Custody of the Registrar-General of Births, Deaths, and Marriages*, there are others which were not surrendered, partly because of the deep independence of spirit of many custodians and partly because registration was often done in Church Books which also included minutes and other records.

Indeed, these records were not always kept in the church buildings, but in the private homes of church officers. Some of these non-surrendered records have found their way to county record offices, to Baptist Church House, London (these records were removed to Regent's Park College, Oxford, in 1985), or to other repositories held by Baptist Theological Colleges or to area Associations of Baptist churches. Yet others are in the hands of the Strict Baptist Historical Society or the Gospel Standard Baptist Library, whilst some still remain in the custody of the churches to which they relate.

Since there is, as yet, no index of the whereabouts of the records of individual churches, and there is such a vast holding at the Public Record Office, search should begin there.

There is another important source of information for the period before 1837. Recognising that the Dissenters kept their own registers in a somewhat sporadic way, the Protestant Dissenting Deputies, a body that existed to protect the civil rights of the Dissenters, established a 'General Register of the Births of the Children of Protestant Dissenters of the three Denominations' (Baptist, Congregational and Presbyterian). This register of births is indexed, and commenced in 1742 (with entries for 1716 and onwards), and continued to 31 December 1837. It is now in the custody of the Public Record Office under the title of its former location, Dr Williams's Library, Red Cross Street, London [PRO reference RG 4/4666-73]. Although centralised in London, it was not limited to Londoners or to Protestant Dissenters; its tens of thousands of entries include some from outside the British Isles, and represented a considerable number of children of Baptist parents.

MARRIAGES

The history of the marriage ceremony among Baptists, as with all Dissenters, falls into three main parts: from 1688 to 1753, from 1753 to June 1837, and since 1 July 1837. During the first period, Dissenting marriages were tolerated, though not legalised as such; in the second period they were neither tolerated nor legalised; in the third they were legalised but under conditions involving a series of stigmas and disabilities which were only removed piecemeal by steady pressure for some sixty years.

Until the passing of Lord Hardwicke's Act in 1753, marriage in Nonconformist chapels was not uncommon, for the public contract made by the parties constituted a legal marriage, though the validity of the ceremony itself was not recognised by the law. The Act, which was occasioned by the scandals of prison weddings and other irregularities was aimed not at Dissenters' marriages but at clandestine marriages. However, by making all marriages illegal in England except those regularly celebrated by the clergy of the Established Church, it removed the old common law toleration of 'irregular' marriages.

During the second period, then, Dissenters were compelled to go the Church of England (or over the border to Scotland!) if they wished to be married legally. But the clergy were not always willing to marry them, especially if they were brought up as Baptists and had not been baptised as infants.

In the third period, although Nonconformist ministers could conduct the ceremony, the attendance of the local civil registrar was required as the 'leading person' responsible for legal formalities and certification. It was not until 1898 that an 'authorised person' who need not be the minister, was allowed to act in the place of the Registrar.

To discover evidence of a Baptist marriage one needs to remember that there are no Nonconformist records before 1642 and few Baptist records before 1688. From 1688 to 1753, there are very few Baptist marriages recorded and from 1753 to 1837, the parish registers of the Church of England are also the most likely source.

For marriages since 1 July 1837 the information obtainable from the General Register Office can scarcely be supplemented.

DEATHS

Parish registers of burials do not usually quote the date of death. Consequently, although the dates of death and burial are generally closer together than many dates of birth and infant baptism, the searcher needs to note that there is a time difference and accordingly a precise date of death is often not available.

Burials took place in parish churchyards except where Baptist meeting-houses had their own burial grounds. Normally, burials were recorded in parish registers when the dead were buried in the churchyard, and quite often when they were not. Anglican officials claimed that, in whatever ground the burial might be, they ought not to be defrauded of their customary fees when funerals occurred in the parish: for example, when, in 1806, the mother of a Dissenting minister at Godmanchester near Huntingdon was buried in a meeting-house ground, 'the Rev. Mr. Harris, a Dissenting minister from Cambridge, delivering an oration at the grave' a fee was demanded by the clergyman [and refused, on the advice of the Protestant Dissenting Deputies!].

In the country many Baptist churches had their own burial grounds, usually adjacent to or surrounding the church; sometimes interments occurred within the church, 'beneath the pulpit' being a not uncommon resting-place for ministers. In urban areas too, burial facilities were sometimes provided within the confines of the church building itself; such burials were termed 'intra-mural' and often the number of burials far exceeded the demands of the membership. Most chapels levied a scale of fees which were greater for non-members, and such burials provided a source of income to the church.

One infamous example was Enon Baptist Chapel, Clement's Lane, Strand, London WC2, of which the Revd William House was minister from 1821 to 1835. This was registered for below-floor burials 1823-42, and more than 1,200 were buried there. The chapel was closed in 1842, bought by a speculator and turned into a dance hall, who issued an advertisement 'Enon Chapel - Dancing on the Dead. Admission threepence. No lady or gentleman admitted unless wearing shoes and stockings.' In 1848 the chapel became the property of a philanthropic surgeon who had all the bodies removed to Norwood Cemetery.

Apart from individual chapel burial grounds, there was a large burial ground for Nonconformists at Bunhill Fields, City Road, London EC1. The Bunhill Fields register, recording interments there from 1713 to 1854 contains over 100,000 (indexed) entries in 33 volumes, and is deposited at the Public Record Office (PRO reference to the indexes is RG 4/4652-57).

Biographical details of some hundreds of these, including many Baptists, are to be found in:

Jones, J A,   *Bunhill Memorials* (London, 1849)
Light, A W,   *Bunhill Fields* (vol. 1, 2nd edn., London, 1915, vol. 2, London, 1933)

Many Baptist chapel burial registers covering the period before 1837 are deposited in the non-parochial registers at the Public Record Office. Although records of deaths since 1 July 1837 are exhaustively covered by the Registrar-General, non-parochial registers for this period are much harder to trace. Some are still in the custody of the individual churches, some are in county record offices and some which had fallen into private hands are without trace. Fortunately, however, all these events are covered by the Registrar-General's registers of deaths.

The rapid rise of the population of England and Wales in the early nineteenth century (1801 = 9 million; 1811 = 10m; 1821 = 12m; 1831 = 13.9m; 1841 = 15.9m; 1851 = 17.9m) meant a continuing increase in the number of births, marriages and deaths, and especially in cities and large towns. One consequence of this is that the urban burial grounds of the Established Church and the Dissenters alike reached saturation point around the middle of the century, and thus urban burials from about 1850 have principally been in municipal cemeteries whose records are kept by the local authorities' registrars of cemeteries. Although these records duplicate some of the information a death certificate would give, they sometimes reveal the existence of relatives buried in the same grave, or indicate there is a memorial which may yield genealogical information.

CENSUS RECORDS

With the exception of the year 1941 (during the Second World War), a decennial census of population has been taken continuously from 1801 to 1991. The first four censuses are only of value for general statistical purposes, but in 1841 the census included names of householders and occupants, a rough indication of age, and relationship to the head of each household of every member of the population, together with an indication of whether or not the subject was born in the county in which he/she resided at census-time. This census was completed in pencil, not always easy to decipher. From 1851 onwards, censuses were completed in ink, gave specific age and birthplace, as well as occupation, and are much more legible. No census returns within the previous hundred years are available for search at the Public Record Office, Chancery Lane, London WC2A 1LR, where these records are kept, the censuses of 1841, 1851, 1861, 1871, 1881 and 1891 being currently available. Indexes have been compiled of the names contained in the census returns for numerous places, so a preliminary search in local libraries could well save a journey to the PRO. The very nature of the census links individuals within families and thus is of prime usefulness to genealogists and family researchers.

Uniquely, in 1851, in addition to the population census, a religious census was held, and every known church, chapel and meeting-place in England and Wales had to complete a standardised form giving church attendance on 30 March 1851, together with the date of foundation of the church and its seating capacity. The form also invited remarks, which are sometimes quite revealing. These returns were all signed by the minster or a lay leader within the church and when used in conjunction with the 1851 population census, can shed further light upon these individuals. The returns of the 1851 religious census are also held by the Public Record Office, Ruskin Avenue, Kew, Surrey TW9 4DU, in class HO 159.

BAPTIST MINISTERS

Unlike such centrally organised denominations as the Church of England, the Methodist Church, or the Salvation Army, there has never been in the Baptist denomination a single repository which even lists all past and present Baptist ministers, much less can give detailed biographical information concerning them. This is a necessary result of the autonomy of each local congregation.

There are some Baptist Ministers, and churches too, which are not allied to any association, union, or grouping with other ministers and churches, but those who are aligned in such a way may currently belong to one of these organisations:

The Baptist Union of Great Britain (formed 1812), Baptist House, P.O. Box 44, 129 Broadway, Didcot, Oxfordshire OX11 8RT. They currently publish *The Baptist Union Directory*, listing ministers and churches in Baptist Union membership. This has appeared annually since 1973. Its forerunners were *The*

Baptist Handbook, 1861-1972, The *Baptist Manual*, 1845-59, and *Account of the Proceedings of the Annual Sessions of the Baptist Union*, 1832-44.

The Baptist Union of Wales (formed 1866), Ilston House, 94 Mansel Street, Swansea SA1 5TU. They publish an annual *Diary and Handbook*.

The Baptist Union of Scotland (formed 1869), Baptist Church House, 14 Aytoun Road, Pollokshields, Glasgow G41 5RT. They publish *The Scottish Baptist Year Book*.

It should be noted that Welsh and Scottish information was included in the Baptist Union publications until very recent times. Many of the churches in membership with the Baptist Unions of Wales and Scotland are also in membership with the Baptist Union of Great Britain, and their information occurs in the publications of both Unions.

The Baptist Union of Ireland, 3 FitzWilliam Street, Belfast BT9 6AW.

Grace Baptist Assembly (Secretary Mr K A Johns, 2a Beechwood Road, Caterham, Surrey CR3 6NA.) The Grace Magazine *Directory of Churches* is published annually and is obtainable from Mr D J Knights, 68 Tupwood Lane, Caterham, Surrey CR3 6DP.

Association of Grace Baptist Churches (South-East) (Secretary Mr M Wade, 139 Grosvenor Avenue, Highbury, London N5 2NH.)

Association of Grace Baptist Churches (East Midlands) (Secretary Mr P Muldoon, 3 Ascendale, Deeping St James, Peterborough, Cambs. PE6 8NZ.)

Association of Grace Baptist Churches (East Anglia) (Administrator Mr D J Piper, Dunoon, Top Road, Rattlesden, Bury St Edmunds, Suffolk IP30 0SJ.)

The Gospel Standard (Strict Baptist, formed 1835) 'List of Chapels and Ministers' Engagements' is published monthly in the *Gospel Standard*. The current producer of this list is Mr J A Hart, 3 Ridings Mead, Chippenham, Wiltshire SN15 1PG.

The Old Baptist Union (formed 1880) (Administrator Revd A H Sommers, 32 Wessex Gardens, Totley Brook, Sheffield S17 3PQ.) Current membership about thirteen churches and one in the Netherlands. Most of these churches joined the Baptist Union of Great Britain in November 1993, and are now formed as an Association within it.

General Baptist Assembly [Inc] (Secretary Mr L J Maguire, 54 Croham Valley Road, South Croydon, Surrey CR2 7NB.)

Some Baptist ministers and churches are in membership of the Fellowship of Independent Evangelical Churches, 3 Church Road, Croydon, Surrey CR0 1SG.

This list does not claim to be complete, but it does give some idea of the diversity of attachment and association of the various churches and ministers, all calling themselves 'Baptist'.

It will be noted that most of the organisations mentioned date from the nineteenth century. The sources of information concerning Baptist ministers and churches of the seventeenth and eighteenth centuries are diverse and include 'Church Books' as the minute books of the churches were generally called, the non-parochial registers, many of which are in the Public Record Office, to which reference has already been made, and the church histories, memorials and monumental inscriptions on gravestones, where these are still extant. Here the county record offices can often help with local background information which adds much interest to the research.

There have been several attempts to list Baptist ministers:

In 1715, Dr John Evans, a Presbyterian, compiled lists of Dissenting congregations in England and Wales, by counties, with names of ministers and some additional information. These lists, with corrections and additions down to 1729, are held by Dr Williams's Library, 14 Gordon Square, London WC1H 0AG, under library reference MS.35.4.

In 1753, the Revd John Collett Ryland wrote an account of the Baptist churches in London, etc. This is to be found in the Warwick Baptist Church minute book, written by Ryland himself when he was minister there. This contains biographical information of 146 Particular Baptist ministers, and a transcript appears in *Transactions of the Baptist Historical Society*, vol. 6 (1919) pp. 138-57. This is the first part of an article entitled 'Baptist Ministers in England about 1750 A.D'; the second part (on pages 157-62) gives a list of General Baptist ministers.

In 1763, the Particular Baptist Fund in London printed a list of Baptist churches and minsters in England, arranged by counties. Based upon Ryland's list of 1753, it included information from other sources. A transcript of this list appears in Ivimey, J, *A History of the English Baptists*, vol. 4 (1830) pp. 13-21.

In 1773, the Revd Josiah Thompson, a Baptist, produced lists (similar to Dr John Evans' of 1715) by counties, for the years 1715 and 1773. These are available in Dr Williams's Library, reference MS.35.5.

From 1790 to 1802, Dr John Rippon produced one of the earliest Baptist periodicals, entitled *The Baptist Annual Register*, which ran to four volumes. During this period, he produced three lists, by counties, of the Particular Baptist churches in England and Wales, with their ministers. The 1790 list appears in vol. 1 on pages 3-16. the 1794 list is in vol. 2, pp. 1-24, and that for 1798 in vol. 3, pp. 1-43. There is a wealth of biographical information in the footnotes to these lists, as well as biographical studies and obituaries elsewhere in this work.

Walter Wilson (1781-1847) produced in four volumes published between 1808 and 1814 *The History and Antiquities of Dissenting Churches and Meeting Houses in London, Westminster and Southwark, Including the Lives of their Ministers*, which, although geographically restricted contains valuable biographies of many Baptist ministers.

The *Baptist Magazine*, which began in 1809, continued from time to time, listings in the same form as Rippon. These are:
1811, pp. 458-63 (England); pp. 496-97 (Wales)
1823, pp. 23-29, 159-62, 331-32, 432-34 (England only)
1827, pp. 32-35, 80-83, 135-39 (England only)
1831, pp. 160-64, 203-07, (England); pp. 499-503 (Wales); pp. 503-04 (Scotland); pp. 590-97 an alphabetical list of Particular Baptist ministers in England; p. 598 General Baptist ministers in England; p. 599 list of Baptist missionaries.
1835, pp. 549-66 Evangelical Baptist churches in England (includes both Particular and General).

The New Baptist Miscellany contains on pages 23-32 of the 1831 volume, a 'List of Baptist Churches [at the end of 1830] with the date of their commencement, the names of their ministers, and the year of their settlement'.

It will be noticed that there is a list of General Baptist ministers (of the New Connexion) in the 1831 *Baptist Magazine*. The General Baptists had two able historians who produced works which list all the General Baptist churches of the New Connexion and their ministers, and contain a wealth of biographical material. These are:

> Taylor, Adam, *The History of the English General Baptists* (2 vols., London, 1818)
>
> Wood, J H, *A Condensed History of the General Baptists of the New Connexion* (London, 1847)

The New Connexion of General Baptists published Minutes of their Annual Associations from 1770 to 1869. This title was then changed to *The General Baptist Year Book*, which appeared annually from 1870 to 1891. All of these contain valuable listings of ministers and churches.

The Minutes of the General Baptists who did not join the New Connexion contain much useful information about churches, as well as their ministers and lay delegates, in Whitley, W T, *Minutes of the General Assembly of the General Baptist Churches in England, 1654-1728 and 1731-1811* (2 vols., London, 1909-10).

Although during the period 1832-44, an *Account of the Proceedings of the Annual Sessions of the Baptist Union* was published each year, lists of churches and ministers appeared only in those for the years 1836, 1838, 1840 and 1843. This publication changed its title to *A Manual of the Baptist Denomination*, and lists of churches and ministers appeared annually from 1845 to 1859.

No annual alphabetical list of ministers appeared during the twenty years following that in the *Baptist Magazine* for 1831. However, production of this list was resumed in the December Supplement to the *Baptist Magazine* for 1851 and this practice continued annually until 1860.

The *Baptist Handbook* which began in 1861 appeared annually until 1972 after which it changed its name to the *Baptist Union Directory*, and is still published.

This contains a list of churches, by counties (latterly Baptist Association Areas) and also ministers, alphabetically.

The Baptist Historical Society maintains a consolidated list of all the obituaries which have appeared in the *Baptist Union Directory*, the *Baptist Handbook*, the *Manual of the Baptist Denomination*, the *Account of the Proceedings* and some of those which have appeared in the *Baptist Magazine*. Application should be made to the Secretary.

There are other listings of ministers to which reference may usefully be made; the Baptist Theological Colleges have all, at some time, published lists of former students, and these usually state the student's home church, his date of joining or leaving college and his location when the list was published.

Although earlier listings did not include this information, one may find what college, if any, a minister attended, from any *Baptist Handbook* issued in 1869 or subsequently.

Many of the listings already mentioned include the name of the county or area Association to which a church belongs. Each of these Associations publishes an annual *Yearbook* or *Handbook* which contains statistical information concerning churches and ministers. Although much of this is duplicated in the national listings, they sometimes provide additional facts.

The Baptist Missionary Society was formed in 1792, and a list of missionaries from the formation of the Society was issued as an appendix to the Centenary volume of the Baptist Missionary Society, published in 1892. This list is on pages 313-29.

Quite a number of ministers also wrote books and some of them, hymns. There are standard dictionaries of hymnology, of which that by J Julian is best known, and many hymnbooks have a companion volume which gives biographies of the writers.

Amongst the works of Baptist bibliography, two stand pre-eminent:

> Whitley, W T, *A Baptist Bibliography:* vol. 1 1526-1776 (London, 1916), and vol. 2 1777-1837, with addenda from 1613 (London,

1922). These books have been out of print for many years but were re-published in one volume in 1985. A third volume was projected, but never published.

Starr, E C,   *A Baptist Bibliography*, 25 vols. (American Baptist Historical Society, Rochester, New York, U.S.A., 1947-76).

CHURCH MEMBERS

Apart from the information in the non-parochial registers, in the Public Record Office, of which a complete list of the Baptist ones is given in Appendix 1, the Church Minute Books of each church, if available, are an important source of information. Nevertheless, in these, Christian names are usually given as initials or omitted altogether, and are only included with reference to some specific action performed by, or required of, the individual concerned. This generally means that only a small minority (often the most vocal!) have their names recorded in the minutes.

Church Books, however often contain a membership list, which can be most useful, as there is sometimes an address or an indication of married surnames of ladies whose membership started when they were single.

The first place to seek a Church Book is in the church itself, failing which the local reference library or county record office. Some records have been deposited with area Associations, and many are in Baptist Theological College libraries and the libraries of the Strict Baptist Historical Society and that of the Gospel Standard Baptists. All those formerly with the Baptist Union are now at Regent's Park College, Pusey Street, Oxford OX1 2LB.

A word of caution is necessary here; where church records are deposited with college libraries, staffing levels do not usually permit their availability for genealogical research. Regrettably, many Church Books have, over the centuries, fallen into private hands and some have been lost.

Individual church members do, however, find mention in many of the Baptist periodicals of which a significant number is detailed in Taylor, R, *English Baptist Periodicals, 1790-1865*, originally published in the *Baptist Quarterly*, vol. 27 (April 1977), pp. 49-82. A further reprint of this article is still available (1994) from the Treasurer of the Baptist Historical Society at £1 plus postage (The Revd T S H Elwyn M.A., B.Sc, B.D., 28 Dowthorpe Hill, Earls Barton, Northampton, NN6 0PB). In addition to periodicals mentioned earlier in this booklet, the *Baptist Times*, published weekly, contains many details of church members.

A most valuable compendium is the *National Index of Parish Registers*, under various general editors, and published in several volumes by the Society of Genealogists. Not all the volumes have been published, but those so far issued are:

vol. 1	General Sources before 1837 [out of print]
vol. 2	Nonconformist Sources [out of print]
vol. 3	Roman Catholic and Jewish Genealogy
vol. 4	Part 1 Surrey [parts relating to Kent and Sussex are out of print]
vol. 5	Gloucestershire, Herefordshire, Oxfordshire, Shropshire, Warwickshire and Worcestershire [out of print]
vol. 6	part 1 Staffordshire
vol. 6	part 2 Nottinghamshire
vol. 7	Cambridgeshire, Norfolk, Suffolk
vol. 8	part 1 Berkshire
vol. 8	part 2 Wiltshire
vol. 9	part 1 Bedfordshire, Huntingdonshire
vol. 9	part 2 Northamptonshire
vol. 9	part 3 Buckinghamshire
vol. 9	part 4 Essex
vol.11	part 1 Northumberland and Durham [out of print]
vol.12	Scottish Genealogy and Family History [out of print]
vol.13	Parish Registers of Wales (does not include nonconformist material)

The second volume, *Sources for Nonconformist Genealogy and Family History,* is especially useful in suggesting lines of approach.

There are now many local and regional family history societies producing literature and offering guidance to the amateur. The Society of Genealogists could direct you to the most appropriate local family history society.

Often, the published histories of individual churches give useful information about ministers and members. The most accessible collection of these histories is to be found at Dr Williams's Library, London, which, in 1973, published a list of them in *Nonconformist Congregations in Great Britain*.

Not all Baptists stayed within the shores of the United Kingdom, and many ministers and members emigrated. The *Baptist Handbook* during the period 1879-1916 contained lists of overseas churches and ministers. The tracing of Baptists who emigrated to the Americas or Australasia is possible through the emigration lists published. Various lists of passengers who settled in the English colonies in America have been published.

There was a considerable Welsh emigration in the early and late eighteenth century, which has been carefully studied, and again lists are available. As they hold a large number of published emigration lists, any enquiry concerning emigrants should first be directed to the Society of Genealogists, 14 Charterhouse Buildings, Goswell Road, London EC1M 7BA.

Finally, careful reading of Cox, J and Padfield, T, *Tracing Your Ancestors in the Public Record Office* (4th edition, 1990), published by HM Stationery Office, will save much time and wasted effort and possibly suggest further avenues of enquiry.

Those whose interest in Baptist history has been awakened may wish to extend their knowledge by joining one or both of the historical societies:

The Baptist Historical Society (formed 1908): Secretary, Revd S L Copson, B.A., MLitt., 9 Silver Birch Road, Erdington, Birmingham B24 0AR.

The Strict Baptist Historical Society (formed 1961): Secretary, Revd K Dix, 38 Frenchs Avenue, Dunstable, Beds. LU6 1BH.

APPENDIX 1

A COMPLETE LIST OF
THE BAPTIST REGISTERS AND RECORDS
IN THE CUSTODY OF THE PUBLIC RECORD OFFICE
CHANCERY LANE, LONDON WC2A 1LR

ENGLAND

The numbers in the first column are the former given numbers of each register.

The W numbers in square brackets in the third column relate to the number allocated to the chapel in Whitley, W T, *The Baptists of London* (London 1928).

* The foundation dates are as stated in the Certificate to the Commissioners when the registers were originally surrendered.

		Founded*			RG 4/
	BEDFORDSHIRE				
4	BEDFORD				
	Mill Street	1796	Births	1792-1837	273
7	BIGGLESWADE	1771	Births	1762-1837	
			Burials	1786-1829	} 309
9	BLUNHAM	1724	Births	1709-1837	
			Burials	1793-1828	} 311
10	CARDINGTON				
	Cotton End Chapel	1777	Births &		
	Independent & Baptist		Baptisms	} 1784-1837	274

11	CRANFIELD	1662	Births	1799-1837	
		Dissolved, and	Burials	1794-1837	220
		reformed 1776			

12	DUNSTABLE	1801	Births &		
	and HOUGHTON				
	REGIS	1804	Burials	1769-1836	221
	formerly THORN	1751			

16	LUTON	1670	Births	1772-1837	
			Burials	1785-1837	276
			Burials	1837-54	90

18	MAULDEN				
	Independent	1700	Births	1730-1837	
	and Baptist		Burials	1785-97	227

| 20 | RIDGMONT | 1811 | Births | 1761-1837 | |
| | | | Burials | 1828 | 228 |

| 22 | SHEFFORD HARDWICK | 1825 | Birth | 1828-36 | 229 |

| 24 | SOUTHILL | 1693 | Births | 1783-1837 | |
| | | | Burials | 1802-20 | 279 |

| 26 | WESTONING | 1816 | Births | 1798-1837 | 91 |

| 28 | WOOTTON | 1828 | Births | 1823-36 | 2392 |

BERKSHIRE

1	ABINGDON				
	Lower Meeting House,	1640	Births	1764-67	
	Ock Street		Burials	1764-89	231
			Births	1786-1824	
			Burials	1785-1828	280
			Births	1797-1837	
			Burials	1828-37	312

14 NEWBURY

Northcroft Lane	1700	Births &		
Meeting House		Baptisms }	1712-1824	87
		Births &		
		Burials	1824-37	286
		Baptisms	1835	86

18 READING

King's Road	Reign of	Births	1819-37	287
Meeting House,	Henry VIII	Burials	1785-1835	1761
formerly				
Hosier's Lane				

26 WALLINGFORD

Thames Street	1794	Births &		
		Baptisms }	1794-1816	237
		Baptisms		
		& Burials }	1814-37	288

BUCKINGHAMSHIRE

1 AMERSHAM

Lower Meeting House	1783	Births	1773-1837 }	
		Burials	1784-1837 }	239

9 CHALFONT ST PETER

Gold Hill Chapel	1780	Baptisms	1782-1802 }	
		Burials	1782-89 }	243
		Births	1779-1836	412
		Burials	1821-36	413

11 CHENIES

	1760	Births	1783-1812 }	
		Burials	1787-1812 }	244

13	CHESHAM				
	Old Meeting House	1719	Births & Baptisms	1783-1823	249
			Births	1823-36	2662
			Burials	1810-27	2093
			Burials	1828-37	252
			Burials	1837	251
14	CHESHAM				
	Blucher Street	1710	Births & Baptisms	1786-1802	2399
19	HADDENHAM	1810	Burials	1823-37	2088
24	NEWPORT PAGNELL				
	Lower Meeting	Reign of Charles II	Births	1810-37	147
25	OLNEY	1694	Births	1789-1837	257
26	PRINCES RISBOROUGH				
	Upper Chapel	1707	Births	1804-37	148
29	WESTCOTT				
	parish of Waddesdon	1833	Births	1834-37	259
30	WINGRAVE				
	Independent and Baptist		Births & Baptisms	1817-37	260

CAMBRIDGESHIRE

9	CHATTERIS				
	Mill End	1778	Births & Baptisms	1778-1821	2252
17	GAMLINGAY	1710	Births	1815-36	151

19	ISLEHAM		1812	Births	1789-1837	152

23 MARCH, ISLE OF ELY
    Bevill's Chapel   1807   Births   1805-37   153
    Calvinistic Baptist

24 MARCH   1700   Births   1798-1837   154
    [also 32 separate Certificates, signed by witnesses, relating to 32 of the above entries]

30 WHITTLESEY, ISLE OF ELY
    1821   Births   1810-37   3541

31 WISBECH
    Ely Place   about time of   Deaths & }
    Protectorate   Burials }   1818-37   2253

32 WISBECH
    St Peter's   1794   Births }
    Upper Hill Street,   Deaths & }   1790-1836   1880
    late Ship Lane   Burials }

34 WISBECH
    Unitarian Baptist   Births   1783-1837 }
    St Peter's,   Burial   1831 }   3362
    Church Lane,
    formerly Dead Man's Lane

CHESHIRE

52 NANTWICH
    Barker Street   1700   Births   1781-1835   189

67a STALEY BRIDGE: *see* **LANCASHIRE** RG 4/1164, 2439

76 TARPORLEY   1817   Births   1801-36   424

CORNWALL

17	HELSTON				
	Coinage Hall Street	1805	Births	1814-37	427
30	PADSTOW	1834	Births	1836	106
55	SCILLY ISLES				
	St Mary's	1818	Births	1819-37	204
63	TRURO				
	Kenwyn Street	1789	Births	1760-1837	682

CUMBERLAND

11	MARYPORT				
	High Street	1808	Births	1797-1836	836

DERBYSHIRE

19	DERBY				
	Brook Street Chapel	1791	Births	1789-1808	694A
			Births	1809-37	695
38	ILKESTON	1785	Births	1773-1808	} 2156
			Baptisms	}	
			& Burials	1792	
			Births	1807-35	708
47	MELBOURNE	1750	Births	1753-1806	507
			Births	1786-1837	945
			Births	1809-37	946
			Burials	1792-1837	118
61	WIRKSWORTH	1816	Births	1802-37	3519

DEVONSHIRE

1 APPLEDORE
   Ebenezer Chapel   1835   Births   1831-37   950

- ASHWATER   Births   1828-37
                               [Unauthenticated Register RG 8/5]

15 BAMPTON
   High Street   1690   Births   ⎫
                               Baptisms   ⎬   1807-36   957
                               & Burials ⎭

7 BARNSTAPLE
   Ebenezer Chapel   1817   Births   1821-37   953

13 BOVEY TRACEY
   Hen Street Chapel   1773   Births &   ⎫
                               Burials   ⎬   1778-1833   956

17 BRAYFORD   1820   Births   1831-37   607

33 CROYDE   1824   Births   1821-35   944

34 CULMSTOCK
   Prescott Meeting   1718   Births &   ⎫
                               Baptisms   ⎬   1787-1836   523

38 DEVONPORT
   Morice Square Chapel 1784   Births &   ⎫
                               Baptisms   ⎬   1770-1837   960

- DEVONPORT
   Morice Square   Baptisms   1785-94   ⎫
                               Burials   1781-1806 ⎭
                               [Unauthenticated Register RG 8/10]

25

43	DEVONPORT				
	Liberty Street and Pembroke Street		Births	1779-1821	963

46	DODBROOK				
	the Refuge Chapel	1819	Births	1824-36	2533

47	EXETER				
	South Street	1600	Births Baptisms & Burials	1785-1837	964

48	EXETER				
	Bartholomew Street	1817	Births	1817-37	335

56	HONITON	1812	Births	1829-37	2027

61	KENTISBEARE				
	Saints Hill Meeting	1814	Births	1806-36	337

62	KINGSBRIDGE	1650	Births & Burials	1785-1831	2099
			Burials	1835-57	442

73	PLYMOUTH				
	How Street Chapel	1637	Births	1786-1837	1215
			Burials	1787-1837	1216

92	STONEHOUSE				
	Ebenezer Chapel, Union Street	1815	Births	1817-37	2854

101	TIVERTON				
	Newport Street	1687	Births	1767-1837	1221
			Burials	1816-37	

DORSETSHIRE

| 15 | LANGTON | 1832 | Births | 1833-37 | 461 |

| 17A | LYME REGIS | 1823 | Burials | 1823-57 | 463 |

| 22 | POOLE | | | | |
| | Hill Street | 1815 | Births | 1797-1837 | 2411 |

35 WEYMOUTH, MELCOMBE REGIS
| | Bank Buildings | 1813 | Births | 1810-37 | 350 |

| 38 | WIMBORNE MINSTER | 1787 | Births | 1778-1834 | 470 |

DURHAM

| 24 | HAMSTERLEY | 1665 | Births & | | |

Baptims } 1750-1837 }
Burials 1785-1837 } 1236

29 MIDDLETON-IN-TEESDALE
| | Hude Street Chapel | 1828 | Births | 1824-36 | 351 |

34 ROWLEY
| | Parish of Muggleswick | 1700 | Births | 1778-1836 | 3557 |

(Also contains entries for two chapels in **NORTHUMBERLAND**)

39 SOUTH SHIELDS
| | Barrington Street | 1818 | Births | 1809-36 | 1096 |

| 50 | SUNDERLAND | 1797 | Births | 1797-1837 | 3556 |

ESSEX

11 CHELMSFORD
| | Duke Street | 1802 | Births & | | |

Namings } 1793-1837 2161

17	COLCHESTER				
	New Meeting,	1814	Births	1798-1837	1507
	Stanwell Street,	dissolved	Burials	1814-37	356
	formerly Baptist	about 1825			
	and Idependent				
20	COLCHESTER	1720	Births	1767-1837 ⎫	
	Eld Lane		Burials	1788-1807 ⎬	1510
			Burials	1816-37	801
31	HARLOW				
		1668	Births	1778-1839 ⎫	
			Burials	1819-37 ⎬	1514
37	LANGHAM	1755	Burials	1782-1826	359
40	LOUGHTON	1817	Births	1820-37	1517
			Burials	1817-37	1518
53	SAFFRON WALDEN	1819	Births	1802-36 ⎫	
	Little Meeting House		Burials	1822-36 ⎬	786
55	SAFFRON WALDEN	1774	Births & ⎫		
	Upper Meeting,		Namings ⎬	1776-1837	1381
	Bailey's Lane		Burials	1821-37	1521
56	SAFFRON WALDEN	1726	Births	1790-1824 ⎫	
	Little Meeting		Burials	1791-1822 ⎬	785
			Births	1826-37	784
			Burials	1827-37	783
67	THORPE-LE-SOKEN	1802	Births	1798-1837	2420
72	WALTHAM ABBEY	1729	Births	1799-1818 ⎫	
	Paradise Row		Burials	1825-37 ⎬	2291
			Deaths	1770-1831	778
			Burials	1836-37	2292
			Burials	1845-57	1383

GLOUCESTERSHIRE

6 BLAKENEY   1833   Burials   1834-37   3568
                                      The births have been registered at Dr
                                      Williams's Library

7 BOURTON-ON-THE WATER
                               1650   Births   1726-1836 ⎫
                                      Burials   1801-36   ⎭ 384

14 CHIPPING CAMDEN   Births   1785-1837 ⎫
                                      Baptisms   1729-66   ⎭ 773

16 CIRENCESTER   1651   Births &   ⎫
   Coxwell Street   Baptisms   ⎬ 1651-1837 ⎫
                                      Burials   1736-1839 ⎭ 3756

22 EASTCOMBE
   Stroudwater   1800   Births   1797-1824   2296

30 HAWKESBURY   1730   Births   1785-1837 ⎫
   Hillsley Street   Burials   1767-1837 ⎭ 2104

31 HORSLEY
   Shortwood   1715   Births   1749-87   2297
   Meeting House   Births   1787-1806   767

49 STOW-ON-THE-WOLD   1716   Births   1821-37   759

50 STROUD   1824   Births   1805-37   621

61 WOOTTON-UNDER-EDGE 1717   Births   1784-1813   3564

HAMPSHIRE

9A CARISBROOKE, ISLE OF WIGHT
                               1809   Burials   1853-58   2107

19	FORTON				
	near Gosport	1811	Births	1799-1836	400

23	HAMBLEDON				
	Anmore Chapel	1827	Births	1820-37	2109

28	LYNDHURST		Births	1783-1810 ⎱	
			Burials	1794-1835 ⎰	2302

32	NEWPORT, ISLE OF WIGHT				
	Castle Hold	1812	Births	1807-37	402

37	PORTSEA				
	White's Row	1782	Births	1817-37	562

39	PORTSEA	1704	Births	1730-1803	1806
	Meeting House Alley		Births	1775-1837	403

44	PORTSMOUTH	1714	Births & ⎱	1785-1837	
	St Thomas		Burials ⎰	1785-1837	2304

51	ROMSEY		Births	1808-37 ⎱	
			Burials	1809-14 ⎰	609
			Burials	1809-36	1397

43	SOUTHSEA				
	Ebenezer Chapel	1813	Births	1808-37	407

59	WELLOW, ISLE OF WIGHT				
		1804	Births	1810-37	1807

HEREFORDSHIRE

3	GORSLEY or LINTON				
	Particular Baptist	1831	Births	1831-37	3571

5	HEREFORD	1828	Births	1831-37	2167

9	KINGTON Lower Chapel, Particular Baptist	1805	Births	1791-1837	1079

13	LEOMINSTER				
	Etnam Street Chapel	1656	Births	1747-1837	} 730
			Burials	1702-1837	
	Etnam Street		Births	1785-92	
	Particular Baptist		Births	1819	} 731
			Burials	1785-93	

17	WESTON-UNDER-PENYARD				
	Ryeford Chapel,	1662	Births	1787-91	2306
	Particular Baptist		Births	1785-1837	} 2909
			Burials	1791-1836	

HERTFORDSHIRE

13	HEMEL HEMPSTED	1731	Births & Baptisms	1785-1827	} 663
			Burials	1785-1824	
			Births	1822-36	664

*	HEMEL HEMPSTEAD Pope's Lane		Births	1824-37	} 665
			Burials	1837	

19	HITCHIN Tilehouse Street		Births Baptisms Marriages Burials	1717-97	} 1808
			Burials	1785-92	
			Births Marriages Deaths	1791-1837	} 667
			Burials	1792-1836	

23	KING'S WALDEN				
	Coleman's Green	1785	Births	1807-37	669

27	RICKMANSWORTH				
	formerly Independent	1827	Births	1823-37	2113
30	ST ALBANS	1675	Births	1822-37	670
	Dagnall Lane		Burials	1822-37	1886
38	WATFORD	1703	Births	1785-1837	} 674
			Burials	1794-1837	

* Supplement between 14/3 and 15/1.

HUNTINGDONSHIRE

1	BLUNTISHAM	1787	Births &		
			Baptisms	1788-1837	}
			Burials	1787-1836	} 626
			Index	1787-1837	3456
3	KIMBOLTON	1692	Births	1799-1836	3757
			A bundle of Certificates		
			corresponding with the		} 32
			above entries		
5	NEEDINGWORTH-cum-HOLYWELL				
		1767	Births	1824-37	677
8	ST NEOTS				
	High Street	1670	Births	1832-35	}
	Independent and Baptist		Baptisms	1802-22	} 3247
9	SPALDWICK	before	Births	1793-1837	3055
		1737	Certificates		22

- **ISLE OF WIGHT**: *see* **HAMPSHIRE**

KENT

- BESSELL'S GREEN: *see* ORPINGTON, RG 4/1728

3 BEXLEYHEATH
    Trinity [W.125]   1827   Burials   1827-37   3891

- BOROUGH GREEN: *see* WROTHAM, RG 4/881

6 BRABOURNE   1818   Births   1817-37   }
    Bethel Chapel   Burials   1819-37   } 679

11 CANTERBURY   supposed Births   1780-1836 }
    Blackfriars   upwards of Burials   1785-1836 } 751
                200 years

16 CHATHAM   1700   Births   1700-1837   755
    Heavyside Lane,   Burials   1785-1837   756
    now Hamond Hill

17 CHATHAM
    Zion Chapel, Clover Street   Burials   1785-1837   916

- CHATHAM
    Providence Chapel, Brook   Births   1814-37
                           [Unauthenticated Register RG 8/13]

20 CRANBROOK   1700   Births   1682-1778 }
                      Burials   1809-37   } 917

35 DOVER
    St Mary's   1643   Births   1730-1837   875

- DOVER
    Pentside Chapel   Births   1809-37
                           [Unauthenticated Register RG 8/15]

40 ERITH   1799   Births   1807-32   }
    Lessness Heath   Burials   1808-23   } 876
    Chapel [W.91a]

42	EYNSFORD [W.83]	1796	Births Deaths & Burials	1799-1837 } 1805-37 }	} 877
43	EYTHORNE	1600	Births Births Births	1723-93 1784-1829 1823-37	703A 1005 878
49	FOLKESTONE	1729	Births	1786-1836	940

47 FOLKESTONE
Zion Chapel,   1786   Births & }
Fenchurch Street,   Baptisms }   1774-1836   1006
formerly Baptist,
but now Countess of Huntingdon's

59	HEADCORN	1755	Births Deaths	1731-1837 1780-1837	932

- LESSNESS HEATH: *see* ERITH, RG 4/876

67	MAIDSTONE				
	King Street	1797	Births	1800-36	935

77 ORPINGTON
   1715 or   Births   1650-1837 }
Bessell's Green,   1667   Burials   1739-1837 } 1728
the Old Meeting House [W.25]

- ROLVENDEN   Births &
                          Baptisms   1796-1834
A facsimile of the original register deposited at Dr Williams's Library, London, may be seen in the Public Record Office at press B.44.

63	ST PETERS				
	Isle of Thanet	1797	Births	1789-1835	2309

83	SANDHURST	1731	Births Burials	1785-1837 } 1786-1837 }	1181

- SELLINDGE: *see* BRABOURNE, RG 4/679

- SELLING: *see* CANTERBURY, RG 4/751

87	SEVENOAKS	1820	Births	1820-34	1184
98	TENTERDEN Honey Lane	1777	Births	1785-1837	1013
102	TUNBRIDGE WELLS Hanover Chapel	1834	Births	1831-37	1757
112	WOOLWICH Enon Chapel	1774	Births	1786-1836	1194
110	WOOLWICH Queen Street Chapel	1788	Births Burials	1781-1836 1821-36	} 1770
114	WROTHAM Borough Green	1817	Births	1818-37	881

LANCASHIRE

1	ACCRINGTON, OLD Lower Chapel	1760	Births Burials	1782-1837 1786-1819	} 1995

- BACUP, Ebenezer Particular Baptist Chapel:
  see ROSSENDALE, RG 4/999, 1731, 1614, 1000, 1001

- BACUP, Irwell Terrace Particular Baptist Chapel:
  see ROSSENDALE, RG 4/1333

15	BLACKBURN Islington	1764	Births Burials	1792-1837 1764-1837	} 1200

26	BOLTON Moor Lane [formerly Scotch Presbyterian]	1821	Births & Baptisms Burials	1793-1836 1813-15	} 1022
34	BURNLEY Sion Chapel, Yorkshire Street	1827	Births	1803-37	2430
45	BUTTERWORTH Rochdale, Ogden Chapel	1780	Births Burials Births Burials Births	1782-1814 1784-1813 1813-25 1814-25 1820-37	} 1029 } 2433 1118
-	CLOUGHFOLD: *see* ROSSENDALE, RG 4/998				
63	COLNE	1788	Births	1776-1836	1033
70	ECCLES	1831	Births	1831-37	2787
75	EVERTON The Necropolis Burial Ground (for all denominations)		Burials	1825-37	3121
96	INSKIP	1817	Births	1812-37	829
102	LANCASTER Bryar Street Scotch Baptist	1809	Births Baptisms	1798-1837 1809-37	} 1475
113	LIVERPOOL Byrom Street	1783	Births Burials	1783-1837 1783-1837	1479
128	LIVERPOOL Lime Street Chapel, formerly in Church Lane, Particular Baptist	1800	Births	1818-37	969

119	**LIVERPOOL** Great Cross Hall Street, Welsh Baptist	1818	Births & Namings	} 1815-37	2557
131	**MANCHESTER** St George's Road, Oxford Street	1790	Births	1777-1836	2692
130	**MANCHESTER** Oak Street, Green Street, General Baptist New Connexion	1824	Births	1819-36	2435
-	OGDEN: *see* BUTTERWORTH, RG 4/1029, 2433, 1118				
159	**OLDHAM** Manchester Street	1815	Births	1816-37	981
180	**PRESTON** Leeming Street Chapel	1782	Births	1782-1836	986
190	**ROCHDALE** Town Meadows Chapel, now West Street Chapel, Particular Baptist	1756	Births Burials	1783-1836 1786-1818	1152
192	**ROCHDALE** Hope Chapel, Hope St. Particular Baptist	1809	Births & Baptisms	} 1805-37	1331
204	**ROSSENDALE, FOREST OF** Cloughfold Meeting House	1700	Births	1811-37	998

207A ROSSENDALE, FOREST OF

Bacup,	1720	Births	1759-88	⎫
Ebenezer Particular		Burials	1783-88	⎬ 999
Baptist Chapel		Births	1787-1816	⎫
		Burials	1788-94	⎬ 1731
		Births	1815-37	1614
		Burials	1782-1806	1000
		Burials	1812-37	1001

207B ROSSENDALE, FOREST OF

Bacup,	1821	Births	1790-1837	1333
Irwell Terrace Particular Baptist Chapel				

209 SABDEN, CLITHEROE

SABDEN, CLITHEROE	1796	Births	1787-1819	⎫
		Burials	1797-1837	⎬ 1122
		Births	1806-37	135
		Births	1833-39	2438

223 STALEY BRIDGE

Ebenezer, Particular	1813	Births	1807-37	2439
Baptist Chapel				

224 STALEY BRIDGE

Mount Pleasant Chapel	1804	Births	1809-37	1164

231 TOTTLEBANK

Ulverston	1669	Burials	1755-1837	3587

LEICESTERSHIRE

2 ARNESBY

formerly at KILBY	1667	Births	1752-1836	1296

6 CASTLE DONNINGTON

CASTLE DONNINGTON	1774	Births &	⎫	
Band Gate Chapel		Burials	⎬ 1785-1835	2446

9 FLECKNEY and SMEATON

General Baptist Chapel	1790	Births	1799-1836	1435

13	HINCKLEY	1763	Births	1776-1836	3187
	Spring Gardens		Supplement-Births	1804-37	2321
	General Baptist				
16	KEGWORTH and DISEWORTH				
		1752	Births	1785-1817	2447
			Births	1813-37	1440
19	LEICESTER				
	Dover Street	1824	Births	1813-37	1442
20	LEICESTER				
	Friar Lane	1688	Births	1802-37	1443
	Meeting House				
21	LEICESTER				
	Upper Charles Street	1831	Burials	1831-37	1125
26	LONG WHATTON				
	General Baptist	1799	Births	1794-1837	1301
	New Connexion				
28	LOUGHBOROUGH				
	Meeting House,	1826	Births	1811-37	27
	General Baptist		Births	1813-37	23
36	MARKET HARBOROUGH				
	General Baptist	1831	Births	1825-37	1458
	New Connexion				
45	QUORNDON formerly with	1770	Births	1760-1836	} 1457
	LOUGHBOROUGH		Deaths & }		
			Burials }	1786-1837	
46	ROTHLEY and SILEBY				
		1800,1818	Births	1791-1836	1307

| 47 SHEEPSHEAD | 1690 | Births | 1754-1837 | } |
| | | Deaths | 1785-94 | } 1456 |

| 49 SYSTON | 1824 | Births | 1827-35 | 1455 |

| 51 THURLASTON | 1813 | Births | 1798-1837 | 1695 |

55 WOODHOUSE EAVES	1796	Births &	}	
		Baptisms	} 1799-1837	}
		Burials	1826-32	} 1312

LINCOLNSHIRE

| 7 BOSTON | 1650 | Births | 1809-37 | 2329 |
| High Street Chapel | | Births | 1785-1830 | 3130 |

6 BOSTON				
High Street,	1786	Burials	1789-94	}
Dissenters'		Burials	1829-37	} 24
Burial Ground		Burials	1837-53	25

| 15 CARLTON-LE-MOORLAND | | | | |
| | 1788 | Births | 1790-1837 | 1888 |

17 FLEET near Holbeach	1709	Births	1709-98	}
		Burials	1709-75	} 1636A
		Births	1780-1826	}
		Burials	1814-37	} 2330
		Births	1709-1837	}
		Burials	1709-77	} 1452
		Marriages	1713-22	}

21 GOSBERTON	1650	Births	1703-1822	}
		Baptisms	1703-27	}
		Burials	1703-1802	} 2829
		Marriages	1717-55	}
		Births	1819-36	1450

23	GREAT GRIMSBY				
	Upper Burgess Street		Births	1833-37	2331
31	LINCOLN	1781	Births	1756-1836	} 1449
	Mint Lane Chapel		Burials	1787-1826	
32	LINCOLN	1701	Births	1816-36	1448
40A	LOUTH	1802	Births	1810-36	} 368
			Burials	1814-37	
44	MONKSTHORP and BURGH		Births	1786-94	} 2457
			Burials	1785-93	
51	SPALDING				
	Enon Chapel	1688	Births	1819-37	367
52	SPALDING				
	Ebenezer Chapel, Love Lane	1766	Births	1807-37	3957
57	STAMFORD				
	Bath Row Chapel	1828	Births	1831-36	4456
59	SUTTERTON	1804	Births	1823-36	369

LONDON AND ENVIRONS (within a radius of four miles from St Paul's)

5	ARTILLERY STREET				
	Bishopsgate, Parliament Court Chapel [W.77]		Births	1791-1811	4369
24	CAMBERWELL				
	Cold Harbour Lane [W.126]	1825	Burials	1825-36	4380
33	CHELSEA				
	Paradise Row [W.108]	1800	Burials	1800-36	4142

39 CHRIST CHURCH
    Church Street [W.72]   1785   Births   1772-1826   4522

46 COMMERCIAL ROAD
    Beulah Chapel,   about the   Births   1787-1837   4268
    St George's East,   time of the
    formerly   Protectorate
    Church Lane, Whitechapel [W.11]

52 DEPTFORD
    Church Street [W.28]   1802   Burials   1824-36   4184

59 EAGLE STREET
    Red Lion Square [W.50] 1737   Births   1770-1813   4235

61 FETTER LANE
    Elim Chapel [W.71]   1790   Burials   1791-1837   4391

83 HENRIETTA STREET
    Brunswick Square   1817   Burials   1828-37   4338
    [W.109]

88 HORSLEYDOWN
    Goat Yard Passage,   1652   Births   1656-1712 ⎫
    then removed to   Marriages   1660-1700 ⎬ 4188
    Carter Lane, Tooley Street   Deaths   1676-1712 ⎭
    and in 1833 to New Park Street, Southwark [W.44]

106 KEPPELL STREET
    Russell Square   1713   Births   1788-1837   4275
    [W.43]

123 MAZE POND
    Southwark [W.34]   1691   Births   1786-1830   4195
                               Burials   1771-1837   4516

130	MILL YARD					
	Goodman's Fields	1600	Burials	1732-83	4505
	[W.13]		Burials	1783-1837	4506

137	OLD FORD					
	Bow [W.73]	1800	Burials	1814-37	4163

152	PRESCOT STREET, LITTLE					
	Goodman's Fields,	1633	Births	1786-1803	4283
	at first meeting				
	in Wapping, then				
	in James Street,				
	Stepney [W.3]				

176	ST LUKE'S					
	Great Mitchell Street	1783	Births	1787-1837	4174
	Meeting [W.70]				

186	WALWORTH	1787	Burials	1813-37	4176
	East Street Chapel[W.79]		Burials	1837-52	4514

192	WILD STREET, LITTLE					
	Lincoln's Inn Fields	1691	Burials	1825-38	4364
	[W.40]		Burials	1835-37	4206

193	WORSHIP STREET					
	Finsbury [W.36]	1779	Burials	1787-1837	4515

MIDDLESEX

9	HAMMERSMITH					
	Trinity Chapel,	1783	Births	1783-1837	}
	West End [W.80]		Burials	1784-1814	} 373
			Burials	1796-1837	2914

13	HARROW-ON-THE-HILL					
	[W.99]	1812	Births	1826-36	1239

MONMOUTHSHIRE

1 ABERGAVENNY
   Frogmore Street   1807   Births   1773-1837   1240

5 ABERSTRWTH
   Hermon Chapel,   1830   Births   1828-36   380
   Nantyglo

4 ABERSYCHAN   1828   Births   1830-37   2463

7 BASSALEG
   Bethel Chapel   Births   1812-37   381

11 CAERWENT   1816   Births   1816-35 ⎫
                                 Burials   1817-35 ⎬   382
                                                     ⎭

23 MYNYDDYSLWYN
   Beulah Chapel   1826   Births   1803-37   630

- NANTYGLO: *see* ABERSTRWTH, RG 4/380

29 NEWPORT
   Commercial Street   1829   Births   1832-37   632

37 RAGLAND
   Ebenezer Chapel   1818   Births   1820-37   1247

41 RHYMNEY
   Iron Works, Penuel   1821   Births   1806-36   634

50 TROSNANT, PONTYPOOL
                          1776   Births   1804-37   635

NORFOLK

1 AYLSHAM   1790   Births   1791-1837 ⎫
                                 Burials   1791-1833 ⎬ 637
                                                       ⎭

3	BACTON	1822	Births	1822-37	} 638
			Burials	1824-36	
8	BUXTON	1796	Births	1794-1837	641
10	DISS	1789	Births	1819-36	1135

| - | DISS, ROYDON and other places in Norfolk and Suffolk | | Births & a few Marriages & Deaths | } 1780-1834 |
| | [Unauthenticated Register RG 8/80] | | | |

13	FAKENHAM	1806	Births	1800-37	644
16	FOULSHAM	1824	Births	1815-37	} 645
			Burials	1823-25	
17	FRAMLINGHAM	1808	Births	1808-36	1136
18	GREAT ELLINGHAM	1699	Burials	1817-37	1254

22	HACKFORD				
	Reepham Chapel	1821	Births	1805-33	} 646
			Deaths	1808-24	

| 24 | HIGHAM, NORWICH | | | | |
| | Rehoboth Chapel | 1824 | Births | 1796-1836 | 647 |

| 26 | INGHAM | | Births | 1770-1837 | } 648 |
| | | | Burials | 1785-1821 | |

- KING'S LYNN: *see* LYNN REGIS, RG 4/1258, 1707

30	LYNN REGIS				
	Stepney Chapel, Broad Street	1760	Births	1789-1837	1258
			Burials	1843-57	1707

36 NEATISHEAD   1811   Births   1801-37 ⎫
                                     Burials   1812-37 ⎬ 650

41 NORWICH
       Priory Yard   1660   Births   1821-36   652

49 NORWICH   1698   Births   1761-1822 ⎫
       St Mary's   Burials   1789-1816 ⎬ 361
                                     Births   1822-37   362
                                     Burials   1816-32   363

49A NORWICH   1778   Births   1784-1838 ⎫
        St Margaret's Chapel   Burials   1789-1856 ⎬ 1785

- REEPHAM: *see* HACKFORD, RG 4/646

- ROYDON: *see* DISS, RG 4/1135 and RG 8/8/80

53 SALEHOUSE
       Particular Baptist   1801   Births   1802-37   2046

54 SAXLINGHAM THORPE
       Particular Baptist   1818   Births   1812-36   1137

55 SHELFANGER   1762   Births   1814-37   1138

65 TITTLESHALL
       Particular Baptist   1823   Births   1826-37   366

NORTHAMPTONSHIRE

1 ALDWINKLE
      St Peter's   1820   Births   1797-1836   1889

4 BLISWORTH   1835   Book of   ⎫
                                    Certificates ⎬ 1794-1836   3360
                                    of Births   ⎭
                                    Deaths   1828-36   3601

46

7	BRAUNSTON	1788	Burials	1827-37	2474
10	BURTON LATIMER	1744	Births	1809-37	893
17	EARL'S BARTON	1793	Births Deaths	1770-1836 1823-37	} 896
20	GRITTON Ebenezer Chapel	1786	Births	1812-37	898
21	HACKLETON	1781	Births Burials	1797-1836 1803-36	890 1140
24	KETTERING Silver Street	1769	Births Burials	1773-1837 1785-1837	} 136
27	KING SUTTON		Births & Baptisms	} 1820-30	2339
28	KISLINGBURY	1810	Births	1809-36	3759
31	MIDDLETON CHENEY Great Chapel		Births Burials	1785-1837 1789-93	} 1274
32	MOULTON	1680	Certificates of Births	} 1795-1836	3361
34	NORTHAMPTON College Street	1785	Births Burials	1786-1837 1786-1837	} 902
43	RINGSTEAD	1714	Births	1792-1836	907
44	ROAD	1720	Births	1816-37	3960

47 THRAPSTON	1787	Births	1783-1837	⎫
		Burials	1793-1837	⎬ 909
		Supplement-Births	⎱	
		& Baptisms	⎰ 1808-31	2918

| 48 TOWCESTER | 1715 | Births | 1755-1836 | 910 |

| 51 WEEDON PINKNEY | 1695 | Births | 1780-1830 | 1280 |

| 58 WEST HADDON | 1821 | Births | 1815-37 | 891 |

NORTHUMBERLAND

12C BERWICK-UPON-TWEED
Calvinistic Baptist,   1804   Births   1805-37   1576
Walker Gate Lane

- BROOMLEY: *see* **DURHAM**, ROWLEY, RG 4/3557

26 NEWCASTLE-UPON-TYNE
Tuthill Chapel   1725   Births   1781-1837   2832

27 NEWCASTLE-UPON-TYNE
New Court Particular   1817   Births   1815-37   2833
Baptist Chapel,
Westgate Street

41 NORTH SHIELDS
Particular Baptist   1799   Births   1790-1837   2835
Baptist Chapel,   [indexed]
Stevenson Street

NOTTINGHAMSHIRE

4 BROUGHTON SULNEY, WIDMERPOOL and
HOSE in **LEICESTERSHIRE**
General Baptist   1800   Births &   ⎱
                            Baptisms   ⎰ 1802-34   2669

7	EAST LEAKE and WIMESWOLD					
	General Baptist	1780	Births	1763-1824		2671
			Births	1775,	}	
				1799-1837		2672

13	KIRBY WOODHOUSE	1746	Births	1748-1836	2485

16	MANSFIELD				
	Stockwell Gate Chapel	1800	Births	1806-37	1584

27	NOTTINGHAM					
	George Street	before 1742	Births	1742-1836	}	
	Chapel, removed		Burials	1785-1837		1351
	from Frair Lane Lane Chapel in 1815					

28	NOTTINGHAM	1775	Births	1784-1830	1589
	Broad Street		Births	1801-37	2676

26	NOTTINGHAM				
	Stoney Street	1799	Births	1809-37	2675
	see also OLD BASFORD, RG 4/2677				

29	NOTTINGHAM				
	Bethesda Meeting,	1828	Births	1806-37	1718
	Barker Gate,				
	Paradise Place				

37	OLD BASFORD				
	and Stoney Street		Births	1801-37	2677
	Chapel, Nottingham				

44	SUTTON BONNINGTON				
	General Baptist	1798	Births	1785-1837	1782
	near Loughborough				

46	SUTTON-IN-ASHFIELD	1760	Births	1760-1810	3603

OXFORDSHIRE

7	BURFORD Witney Street	1700	Births Deaths & Burials	1809-35 } 1830-36	}2051

9	CHIPPING NORTON	1662	Births Births	1767-1830 1767-1830	3763 2845

11	COATE parish of Bampton	1664	Births Burials	1647-1836 1657-1837	 140

20	SYDENHAM	1821	Births & Deaths }	1821-36	2793

21	THAME	1825	Births	1826-37	1601

23	WITNEY Independent and Baptist	1700	Births & Baptisms } Births & Baptisms }	1799-1819 1822-36	2794 1602

RUTLANDSHIRE

2	MOORCOTT and BARROWDEN	1710 & 1806	Births	1769-1837	1811

3	OAKHAM	1772	Births Burials	1766-1837 1786-1827 }	1603

SHROPSHIRE

3	BRIDGNORTH Castle Street Chapel	1705	Births & Deaths }	1779-1836	1605

5	BROSELEY Birch Meadow Chapel	1800	Births	1794-1837	1892

8	CHIRBURY	1829	Births	1827-35	2796
30	PONTESBURY	1826	Births	1828-37	1893
34	SHIFNAL				
	Aston Street	1780	Births	1811-36	1817
36	SHREWSBURY	1620	Births	1766-1825	1819
	Claremont Street		Births	1813-36	2798
	Meeting House				
45	WEM				
	Cripple Street	1813	Births	1823-36	1821

SOMERSETSHIRE

5	BATH	1720	Births	1763-89	3195
	Somerset Street		Births	1784-1836	}
			Burials	1785-1837	1790
19	BRISTOL		Burials	1679-1746	3765
	Broad Mead		Burials	1746-91	2871
			Burials	1789-1803	1826
			Burials	1804-36	1827
			Burials	1836-37	1828
			Burials	1756-1827	1829
			Burials	1825-34	2923
			Births	1787-1817	2697
			Births	1813-37	1358
19A	BRISTOL				
	King Street		Burials	1827-55	2698
31	CHARD	1652	Births	1786-94	34
			Births	1807-37	}
			Burials	1836-37	2689
34	CREWKERNE				
	North Street Chapel	1820	Births	1831-37	2699

44 FROME	1689	Births	1801-37	3261
Badcox Lane		Burials	1785-1827	1550
Meeting House		Burials	1832-37	3264

45 FROME	1707	Births	1785-95	⎫
Sheppard's Barton		Burials	1792-95	⎬ 1551
Meeting House		Births	1802-36	3262
		Burials	1764-1826	2925
		Burials	1750-1837	*3263

* RG 4/3263 includes copies of entries for Meeting House Burial Ground and a few entries relating to St Catherine Hill Burial Ground, 1750-1824, compiled from Sexton's book.

62 PAULTON				
near Bath	1690	Births	1785-1836	⎫
		Burials	1827-36	⎬ 1733

| 65 ROWBERROW | 1814 | Births | 1816-37 | 1559 |

| 74 STOGUMBER | 1726 | Births | 1810-36 | 1565 |

| 75 STREET | 1814 | Births | 1814-37 | ⎫ |
| | closed 1837 | Burials | -1837 | ⎬ 1422 |

| 78 TAUNTON | 1815 | Births | 1782-1837 | ⎫ |
| Silver Street | | Burials | 1823-36 | ⎬ 3219 |

| 76 TAUNTON | | | | |
| Octagon Chapel, Middle Street | 1816 | Births | 1816-26 | 1566 |

83 WELLINGTON	1750	Births	1784-96	⎫
		Burials	1785-93	⎬ 1750
		Births	1781-1837	⎫
		Burials	1809-30	⎬ 1736

| 87 WELLS | | | | |
| Ebenezer Chapel | 1814 | Births | 1814-35 | 2935 |

94 YEOVIL
    South Street Chapel   1688   Births   1810-36   1737

STAFFORDSHIRE

- BRETTELL LANE: *see* KINGSWINFORD, RG 4/3296

6	BURSLEM		Births	1791-1837	3856
10	BURTON-UPON-TRENT				
	Cat Street Chapel before 1800		Births	1793-1836	2129
13	BURTON EXTRA				
	Burton-upon-Trent	1824	Births	1821-37	3363
19	CLENT				
	Holy Cross	1802	Births	1807-36	2718
20	COPPICE, COSELEY	1804	Births &		
			Namings	1794-1819	1868
			Births	1819-37	2719
22	COSELEY				
	Darkhouse Chapel, parish of Sedgley	1786	Births	1791-1837	2803
21	COSELEY	1809	Births &		
	Providence Chapel, parish of Sedgley		Namings	1809-37	3295
29	KINGSWINFORD				
	Brettell Lane	1798	Births	1778-1836	3296
68	WOLVERHAMPTON				
	Walsall Street	1829	Births & Namings	1832-37	1876

SUFFOLK

1	ALDRINGHAM	1812	Births	1812-37	1741
2	BARDWELL	1824	Births	1820-37	2823
5	BECCLES	1805	Burials	1828-37	1833
12	CHELMONDISTON	1824	Births	1810-34	} 1835
			Burials	1831-34	
			Birth Certificates	1831-37	} 3924
14	CLARE	1803	Deaths	1822-35	2127
19	EYE	1810	Births	1805-36	} 3196
			Deaths & Burials	1812-34	
22	FRAMSDEN	1835	Births	1831-37	2355
24	GRUNDISBURGH		Births	1804-35	16
			Births	1816-37	17
25	HADLEIGH				
	George Street	1820	Births	1821-37	1841
30	IPSWICH	1758	Births	1785-1837	1846
	Stoke Green		Burials	1829-37	1847
			Burials	1850-55	2824
32	IPSWICH				
	Dairy Lane	1829	Births	1810-37	1850
42	LOWESTOFT				
	High Street Chapel	1812	Births	1812-28	1429

43	MILDENHALL				
	West Row	1813	Births	1802-37	2705
49	OTLEY	1800	Births	1800-36	1856
55	STRADBROKE	1814	Births	1814-36	2825
58	WALSHAM-LE-WILLOWS	1822	Births	1811-37	2804
59	WALTON	1808	Births	1807-37	2709

Unauthenticated Register RG 8/66 lists Baptist burials at various places in Suffolk, 1780-1834. It also contains a few entries of deaths and a marriage during the above period, and may be seen in the Public Record Office at press No. 69.

SURREY

2	BETCHWORTH				
	Brockham Chapel	1785	Births	1785-1836	3925
11	CHOBHAM				
	West End Chapel	1796	Births	1810-36	1742
13	CLAPHAM				
	Particular Baptist Chapel [W.76]	1777	Births	1781-1835	3059
30	KINGSTON-UPON-THAMES				
	Particular Baptist	1790	Births	1783-1807	2126
	Chapel, Brick Lane		Births	1802-37	3424
	[W.78]		Supplement-Births	1837	2938
			Deaths	1799-1836	3425
45	WANDSWORTH	1821	Births	1816-34	1901
	Particular Baptist Bridge Field Meeting [W.122]		Burials	1825-36	2216

4 BILLINGSHURST
    General Baptist Chapel   Burials   1821-36   2989

7	BRIGHTON	1785	Births	1775-1835	
	Salem Chapel,		Burials	1790-1834	} 2712
	Bond Street		Births	1835-37	2940

22	DITCHLING				
	General Baptist	before 1741	Baptisms	1811-33	1796
	Meeting House		Burials	1821-37	1797

25	HAILSHAM	1794	Births & Namings	} 1794-1837	2622

32	HORSHAM	1700	Births & Baptisms	} 1688, 1706-1836	
	General Baptist		Burials	1771-1836	} 2729
	Chapel		Burials	1721-68	2062

36	LEWES	1776	Births	1788-1837	2966

45	ROTHERFIELD	1774	Births	1828-36	
			Deaths	1784-1829	} 3631

46	RYE	1750	Births	1769-83	
			Burials	1768-1808	} 3365
			Births	1786-1837	
			Deaths	1785-1836	} 2968

- SHOVERS GREEN: *see* WADHURST, RG 4/3366, 2366

50	UCKFIELD				
	Rock Hall	1787	Births	1783-1835	
	Meeting House		Burials	1792-1837	} 2969

51	WADHURST	1815	Births &	}		
	Shovers Green		Baptisms	}	1818-37	3366
			Burials		1832-35	2366

54	WIVELSFIELD	1763	Births &	}		
			Baptisms	}	1790-1837 }	
			Burials		1790-1837 }	2970

WARWICKSHIRE

- ALCESTER: *see* **WORCESTERSHIRE**, FECKENHAM, RG 4/2016

11	BIRMINGHAM	1737	Births	1785-1801	2972
	Cannon Street		Births	1798-1814	3636
			Births	1782-1835	2973
			Births	1799-1837	3114
			Supplement-Births	1817-37	3116
			Burials	1786-94	2972
			Burials	1799-1837	3115

10	BIRMINGHAM	1785	Births	1775-1837 }	
	Bond Street		Burials	1794-1837 }	3113

8	BIRMINGHAM	1786	Births	1786-1808	4109
	Lombard Street		Births	1813-36	1903

12	BIRMINGHAM				
	Zion Chapel,	1796	Births	1821-37	3117
	New Hall Street				

28	COVENTRY	1773	Births	1769-1837 }	
	Longford Chapel		Burials	1801-37 }	2981

29	COVENTRY				
	Cow Lane, formerly	1793	Births	1761-1836	2982
	Jordan Well		[indexed]		

32	COVENTRY General Baptist, Whitefriars' Lane	1825	Births	1826-37	2627
33	DRAYCOTT parish of Bourton	1811	Births & Namings }	1812-37	3202
37	HENLEY-IN-ARDEN	1700	Births	1791-1830	4481
45	MONK'S KIRBY	1817	Births	1805-37	1712
55	WOLSTEN	1810	Births	1811-37	2956

WESTMORLAND

[NONE]

WILTSHIRE

1	ALLINGTON parish of All Cannings	1829	Births	1826-37	2984
13	CHIPPENHAM	1804	Births	1789-1837	2987
17	DEVIZES	16th century	Births Deaths & Burials }	1772-1837 1780-1836 }	2230
22	DOWNTON South Lane Chapel	1738	Births Burials	1800-37 1794-1836 }	2013
24	EAST KNOYLE and SEMLEY	1824	Births	1821-37	4486
32	LUDGERSHALL	1816	Births Births Burials	1817-36 1833-37 1826-35 }	2131 2235

37	MALMESBURY				
	Abbey Row		Births	1794-1837	2238

42	MELKSHAM	1714	Births	1794-1837	} 3043
			Burials	1794-1837	

45	NETHERAVON		Births	1814-37	2241

46	NETTLETON	1826	Births	1827-36	} 2132
			Burials	1826-32	

48	NORTH BRADLEY	1779	Births	1790-1836	3045
			Burials	1779-1837	2242

51	SALISBURY	1688	Births	1785-87	} 2064
	Brown Street		Births	1788-91	
			Births	1763-1837	} 1433
			Burials	1792-1836	

58	TROWBRIDGE				
	Back Street	1737	Burials	1822-37	3047

61	TROWBRIDGE				
	Conigree Chapel	1660	Births	1816-37	2958

64	WARMINSTER				
	Ebenezer Chapel, North Row	1812	Burials	1812-36	2740

WORCESTERSHIRE

- ASTWOOD: *see* FECKENHAM, RG 4/2016

1	BEWDLEY	1649	Births	1776-1836	} 2066
			Deaths &	} 1758-1836	
			Burials	1758-1836	

5	BROMSGROVE Worcester Street, Independent and Baptist	1787	Births & Baptisms Births	} 1785-1804 1804-36	} 2734
7	BROMSGROVE Little Cat's Hill	1820	Births Baptisms Deaths Burials	} 1830-37	2136
9	CRADLEY	1801	Births & Dedications Burials	} 1794-1836 1805-37	} 3371
12	DUDLEY New Street Chapel	1766	Births Deaths	1816-37 1814-37	} 2735
18	FECKENHAM, Astwood Chapel, and Alcester in **WARWICKSHIRE**	1793	Births Deaths Burials	1788-1837 1801-06 1800-37	} 2016 2067
22	KIDDERMINSTER Union Street Chapel	1813	Births	1814-37	2739
30	SHIPSTON-UPON-STOUR	1778	Births	1783-1836	3375
34	TENBURY Cross Street Chapel	1816	Births	1820-36	2068
37	WORCESTER Silver Street Chapel	1712	Births	1793-1837	1908

YORKSHIRE

5	ALMONDBURY Broadlands Chapel	1816	Births	1809-38	3377

22 BARNOLDSWICK

Bridge Chapel	1650	Births	1785-1837	}	3930
		Burials	1786-1834		

23 BEDALE

	1793	Births	1785-1827	}	3381
Ebenezer Chapel		Baptisms	1793-1822		
		Births	1808-27		3382

26 BEVERLEY

Walker Gate Chapel	1791	Births	1787-1836	1909

33 BISHOP BURTON

	1770	Births	1755-1836	}	3223
		Burials	1776-94		

- BOROUGHBRIDGE: *see* DISHFORTH and BOROUGHBRIDGE, RG 4/2997

40 BRADFORD

Westgate Chapel	1753	Births	1784-1837	1910
		Supplement-Births	1812-37	4433

38 BRADFORD

Sion Chapel,	1824	Births	1814-37	2991
Bridge Street		Supplement-Births	1814-37	3385

- BRADFORD: for other Baptist churches, *see* CLAYTON, RG 4/2993, 3025, 3026, 3027, 3516, 3436 and HEATON, RG 4/2142

45 BRAMLEY

the Lane Chapel	1779	Births	1783-1803		3142
		Births	1799, 1803-18	}	3141
		Births & Namings	} 1818-24		1714
		Births	1824-37		2810
		Deaths	1823-37		3321

48	BRIDLINGTON	1698	Births	1698-1783	⎫	
			Marriages	1700-43	⎬ 3019	
			Burials	1700-47	⎭	
			Births	1783-1836	⎫	
			Burials	1783-1837	⎭ 3143	

63	CLAYTON					
	parish of Bradford	1830	Births	1782,	⎫	
				1801-37	⎭ 2993	

64	CLAYTON	1773	Births	1748-1829	⎫	
	Queen's Head Chapel,		Burials	1788-94	⎬ 3025	
	parish of Bradford		Burials	1831-37	⎭	
			Births	1786-1837	3026	
			Births	1766-1837	3027	
			Births	1776-1837	3516	

| 65 | CLAYTON | | | | | |
| | West Chapel | 1821 | Births | 1818-37 | 3436 | |

| 72 | CRIGGLESTONE | 1822 | Births & | ⎫ | | |
| | near Wakefield | | Burials | ⎭ 1822-37 | 4480 | |

85	DISHFORTH and BOROUGHBRIDGE					
	Dishforth and	1816	Births	1819-37	2997	
	Langforth Chapels					

| 92 | EARBY | 1819 | Births | 1802-37 | 1913 | |

| 107 | FARSLEY | 1777 | Births | 1779-1837 | ⎫ | |
| | Rehoboth Chapel | | Burials | 1785-1837 | ⎭ 3160 | |

112	GILDERSOME	1717 or	Births &	⎫		
	Parish of Batley	rather earlier	Baptisms	⎬ 1799-1837	3006	
			[with Index]	⎭		

114	GOLCAR	1836	Births &		
			Namings }	1833-38	
			Burials	1835-37 }	2812

121	GREAT DRIFFIELD	1788	Births	1796-1835	3008

131	HALIFAX	1763	Births	1779-1837	3165
	Pellon Lane Chapel		Deaths & }		
			Burials	1785-1837	3166

- HALIFAX: for other Baptist churches, *see* RISHWORTH, RG 4/2752, 2753
  and WADSWORTH, RG 4/2775, 2776

- HALLIFIELD: *see* HELLIFIELD RG 4/3171

149	HEATON				
	Bethel, or Swaine	1824	Births	1798,	
	Boyd Lane Bottom Chapel,			1807-37 }	2142
	parish of Bradford				

- HEBDEN BRIDGE: *see* WADSWORTH, Birchcliff, RG 4/2775, 2776

141	HELLIFIELD and LONG PRESTON				
		1807	Births & }		
			Baptisms	1803-37	3171

150	HEPTONSTALL				
	Ebenezer Chapel	1777	Births	1745-1837 }	
			Burials	1785-94 }	3176

151	HEPTONSTALL SLACK	1807	Births	1789-1837	3014
	Mount Zion Chapel		Burials	1808-37	2642

164	HORSFORTH				
	near Leeds,	1801	Births	1800-35	3471
	Zion Chapel		Births	1800-37	3136

172 HUDDERSFIELD
   Pole Moor Chapel   1788   Births   1831-37   2814

173 HUDDERSFIELD
   Lockwood Chapel   1795   Births   1792-1837   2744

 - HUDDERSFIELD: *see also* SALENDINE NOOK, RG 4/2748, 2749

180 HULL   1796   Births   1774,   ⎫
   George Street Chapel   1794-1837   ⎬ 3204
                                                               ⎭

183 HULL
   Unitarian Baptist   Births   1801-12   4483

192 HUNMANBY   1817   Births   1786-1836   ⎫
                               Deaths &   ⎫   ⎬ 3227
                               Burials   ⎭   1819-36   ⎭

196 IDLE   1810   Burials   1810-37   79

201 KEIGHLEY   1811   Births   1791-1837   ⎫
   Bethel Chapel   Burials   1830-36   ⎬ 3393
                                                              ⎭

206 KILDWICK   1711   Births   1768,   ⎫
   Sutton Chapel   1785-1837   ⎬ 1915
                               Burials   1785-94   ⎭

207 KILHAM   1820   Births   1821-36   3233

 - KINGSTON-UPON-HULL: *see* HULL, RG 4/3204, 4483

224 LEEDS
   South Parade,   1779   Births   1785-1837   3761
   formerly The Old Baptist Chapel

234A LEEDS
   Ebenezer Chapel   Births   1782-97   ⎫
                               Burials   1786-94   ⎬ 3432
                                                              ⎭

64

- LOCKWOOD: *see* HUDDERSFIELD, Lockwood Chapel, RG 4/2744

- LONG PRESTON: *see* HELLIFIELD RG 4/3171

257 MASBOROUGH   Births   1789-1835   3406

264 MILLWOOD
      Rehoboth Chapel   1808   Births   1699-1832   2649

265 MIRFIELD   1825   Births   1825-37   }
      near Dewsbury   Burials   1833-37   } 1918

276 NEW MALTON
      Salem Chapel   1824   Births   1829-36   2658

- POLE MOOR: *see* HUDDERSFIELD, Pole Moor Chapel, RG 4/2814

301 QUARMBY-cum-LINDLEY
      Salendine Nook   1743   Births &   }
      Meeting House,   Dedications   } 1783-1823   }
      parish of Huddersfield   Burials   1783-94,   } 2748
                                                        1809   }
                                      Births   1820-37   2749

302 RAWDEN   1715   Births   1755-1808   37
      Brixstone Chapel   Births   1783-92   }
                                       Burials   1783-91   } 2080
                                       Births   1780-1817 }
                                       Burials   1793-1818 } 2081
                                       Births   1803-37   }
                                       Burials   1837   } 2815

313 RISHWORTH
      Roadside Chapel,   1802   Births   1802-24   2752
      parish of Halifax   Births   1824-37   2753

- SALENDINE NOOK: *see* QUARMBY-cum-LINDLEY, RG 4/2748, 2749

322	SCARBOROUGH			
	Ebenezer	1771	Births	1767-1834 ⎫
	Meeting House		Burials	1776-1835 ⎬ 3685
353	SKIDBY	1826	Births	1824-36 2764
391	THURLSTONE	1828	Births	1817-37 2614
394	WADSWORTH	1764	Births	1785-1812 2775
	Birchcliff,		Births	1797-1837 ⎫
	parish of Halifax		Burials	1816-37 ⎬ 2776
420	YORK			
	New Jubbergate,	1799	Births	1779-1835 3518
	formerly College			
	Street, then			
	Peasholme Green			

WALES

ANGLESEA

9 BRIENSIENCYN [=BRYNSIENCYN] and PENYCARNEDDI
   The Tabernacle,   1810   Births   1811-37   3547
   Llanidan

16 LLANERCHYMEDD
   Tabernacle,   1817   Births   1805-28   3937
   parish of Amlwch

57 LLANRHYDDLAD
   Rhydwyn Chapel   1802   Births   1789-1836   3791

51 PENYMYNYDD,
   PENYCARNEDDI   1810   Births   1824-37   3790

BRECON

1 BRECON
   Watergate Chapel   1807   Births   1806-37   ⎫
                                Burials   1808,1825   ⎬ 3938
                                                       ⎭

32 TALACHDDU,
   MAESYBERLLAN   1699   Births   1803-37   3941

CARDIGAN

[NONE]

CARMARTHEN

5 CARMARTHEN

The Tabernacle,	1660	Births	1785-1828	}
formerly Dark Gate		Burials	1790-1837	} 3942
		Births	1827-37	4124

7 CARMARTHEN

Penuel Chapel,	1786	Births	1789-1837	4437
Priory Street				

- CWMNFELYN

Llanwnio, Particular Baptist   Births   1779-1828

Unauthenticated Register RG 8/103]

22 LLANELLY

Tynewydd Felinfol	1709	Births	1775-1820	3821

42 LLANGYNOCK

Ebenezer Chapel	1801	Births	1778-1837	3944

CARNARVON

[NONE]

DENBIGH

43 LLANFUROG

Mwrog Street Chapel	1800	Births	1792-1830	3530
		Births	1824-37	4115

71 RUABON

Pen-y-cae	1796	Births	1789-1837	3490

91 WREXHAM

Old Meeting House,	1708	Births	1785-90	}
Chester Street		Burials	1785-91	} 3868
		Births	1790-1837	}
		Burials	1791-94	} 3869

FLINT

31 RHUDDLAN		Births	1815-37	3949

GLAMORGAN

1 ABERDARE

Carmel Chapel	1806	Births	1806-37	} 4117
		Deaths	1814-36	

38 BRIDGEND

Ruhamah Chapel, Newcastle	1789	Births	1799-1837	3502

7 CARDIFF

Bethany Chapel,	1806	Births	1804-16	} 3879
St Mary Street		Deaths	1807-16	
		Births	1804-37	} 3493
		Deaths	1807-37	

27 MERTHYR TYDVIL

Bethel Chapel, Georgetown	1807	Births	1810-37	3499

36 NEATH

Bethany	1770	Births	1773-1837	3950

45 SWANSEA

Mount Pleasant Meeting House	1826	Births	1811-37	3503

44 SWANSEA

York Place Chapel	1830	Births	1801-37	2667

MERIONETH

10 DOLGELLY
Juda, West Street, 1798 Births 1798-1836
Particular Baptist Baptisms 1800-35 } 3898

 - LLANUWCHLLYN Baptisms 1831-33 3898

 - LLYNGWRIL Baptisms 1832 3898

MONTGOMERY

14 LANDRINIO
Sarnwen Chapel 1829 Births 1832-36 3905

10 LLANIDLOES
Particular Baptist 1810 Births 1804-37 3958

PEMBROKE

19 LLANGUM BURTON [= LLANGWM]
Galilee Chapel 1820 Births 1820-36 2491

20 MILFORD
Short Lane Chapel 1828
and Enon, SANDY } Births 1803-36 3476
HAVEN, ST ISHMAEL 1814

 - MOLESTON: *see* NARBERTH, RG 4/3964

22 NARBERTH
Bethesda 1817 Births 1807-37 3963

23 NARBERTH
Moleston Chapel 1768 Births 1787-1837 3964

27 PEMBROKE DOCK
    Bethany Chapel   1818   Births   1814-37   3965

- SANDY HAVEN: *see* MILFORD, RG 4/3476

RADNOR

[NONE]

NOTES

APPENDIX 2

A LIST OF THE ENGLISH AND WELSH BAPTIST REGISTERS INCLUDING PARTICULAR AND UNITARIAN BAPTISTS OF WHICH COPIES ARE HELD IN THE LIBRARY OF THE SOCIETY OF GENEALOGISTS

Compiled by SUSAN GIBBONS

This listing follows the conventions of the Library and its published guides in that county names are those in use before the 1974 reorganisation of local government. In London only places within the City of London are shown; places outside the boundaries of the City are listed under the ancient counties in which they were situated (i.e. Essex, Kent, Middlesex and Surrey), for example Deptford appears under Kent and Southwark under Surrey.

Abbreviations: A=Adult Baptisms; B=Burials; C=Baptisms; D=Deaths; Extr=Extracts; (I)=Index; M=Marriages; R=Infant Naming (Registration or Dedication); Z=Births.

Shelf marks are enclosed in square brackets [ ] and unless otherwise stated the volumes are in the **[R]**egister series for the appropriate county. **[P]** indicates that the entry is to be found in a periodical. **Mf** and **Mfc** are microfilms and microfiche respectively.

ENGLAND

BEDFORDSHIRE

BLUNHAM
Z 1773-74, A 1738-1801,
D 1736-1806, 1860-90, B 1852-90 [37]

BERKSHIRE

FARINGDON (Anabaptist)
B 1678-1766 [59]

BUCKINGHAMSHIRE

CHALFONT ST PETER Gold Hill
Z 1779-1836 [P]

PRINCES RISBOROUGH
Z 1796-1837 [82]

SPEEN, near Aylesbury
Z 1813-37 [82]

CAMBRIDGESHIRE

WILLINGHAM
Z 1781-84, R 1781-1820,
A 1790-1827, D 1728-49 [80]

WISBECH
ZMDB 1700-1838 [117, 160]

CHESHIRE

BRAMHALL
A 1866-76, 1883-92, B 1860-1911 [31]

DUCKENFIELD *see* DUKINFIELD

DUKINFIELD
M 1677-1713 [33]

WARFORD, GREAT
Z 1757-1854, A 1757-1854,
B 1800-59, 1880-1929 [31]

CORNWALL

HELSTON
Z 1805-37 [23]

PADSTOW
Z 1836 [25]

ST MARY, SCILLY ISLES
Z 1819-37 [26]

TRURO
Z 1760-1837 [27]

DERBYSHIRE

WIRKSWORTH
Z 1821-37 [Mf], C 1824-37 [48]

DEVONSHIRE

APPLEDORE
Z 1834-37 [94, Mf]

BAMPTON
Z 1807-37, B 1827 [95, Mf]

BARNSTAPLE
Z 1821-37 [94, Mf]

BOVEY TRACEY
Z 1778-1837, B 1784-1837 [95, Mf]

BRAYFORD
Z 1831-37 [95, Mf]

CROYDE
Z 1821-35 [96]

CULMSTOCK Prescott Chapel
Z 1786-1837 [96], Z 1787-1836,
B 1789-1837 [Mf]

DEVONPORT
Liberty Street or Pembroke Street
Z 1779-1810 [97, Mf];
Morice Sq, Plymouth Dock
Z 1785-1837 [96], Z 1770-1837 [Mf]

DODBROOKE (Refuge)
Z 1819-36 [Mf]

EXETER
Bartholomew Street Z 1817-37 [Mf];
South Street Z 1786-1837,
B 1785-1837 [Mf]

HONITON (Part Bapt)
Z 1829-37 [Mf]

KENTISBEARE Sainthill
Z 1806-36 [Mf]

KINGSBRIDGE
Z 1785-1813, B 1785-1857 [Mf]

PLYMOUTH How Street
Z 1786-1837,
B 1787-1837 [Mf]

STONEHOUSE (Ebenezer)
Z 1833-36 [Mf]

TIVERTON Newport Street
Z 1767-1837, B 1816-37 [Mf]

DURHAM

HAMSTERLEY
C 1729-1848, D 1771-1848 [NU/R 32]

ESSEX

SAFFRON WALDEN (General Baptist
Meeting House) Z 1826-37 [19]

HAMPSHIRE

HAMBLEDON Anmore Chapel
Z 1820-37 [113]

PORTSMOUTH St Thomas Street
Z 1785-1836, B 1788-1832 [114]

HEREFORDSHIRE

GORSLEY (or LINTON)
Z 1831-37 [13]

HEREFORD
Z 1832-37 [13]

KINGTON
Z Extr 1791-1815, Z 1816-37 [13]

LEOMINSTER
Z 1733-1836, B 1702-1837 [13]

WESTON-UNDER-PENYARD
Z 1787-1837, DB 1791-1836 [13]

HERTFORDSHIRE

BERKHAMSTED
Z 1799-1837, B 1801-83 [52]

HATFIELD Park Street (Ind & Bapt
Union)
ZC 1823-54, B 1846-1920 [57]

KENT

BESSELS GREEN (General Baptist) [W.25]
Z 1682-1815, M 1840-53,
DB 1738/9-1861 [227]

BEXLEYHEATH, Trinity [W.125]
B 1827-37 [227]

CANTERBURY (Blackfriars)
Z 1780-1836, B 1785-1836 [227]

CHATHAM Heavyside Lane (General Baptist Church)
Z 1700-1837,
B 1785-1837 [256]

DEPTFORD, Church Street [W.28]
B 1824-34 [Mfc]

ERITH Lessness Heath Chapel [W.91a]

Z 1807-29, DB 1808-22 [231]

EYTHORNE
Z 1723-1837, D 1797-1858 [Mfc]

ROLVENDEN
Z 1796-1834 [234]

LANCASHIRE

ACCRINGTON Machpelah Chapel
B 1834-64 [Mfc]

BLACKBURN Islington (Part Bapt)
Z 1786-1837, B 1764-1837 [Mfc]

HAGGATE
Z 1762-1841, B 1786-94, 1811-57 [Mfc]

PRESTON, LONG
M(I) 1884-1957, B 1836-1985 [Mfc]

LEICESTERSHIRE

LEICESTER
Archdeacon Lane Z 1820-36,
DB 1821-53 [14];
Dover Street Z 1813-37;
Friar Lane Z 1785-1837, B 1787-89;
Harvey Lane Z 1784-1832, B 1805-37 [41];
Upper Charles Street DB 1831-37 [41]

LONDON (CITY of)

BISHOPSGATE
Z 1789-1811 [263]

MIDDLESEX

HAMMERSMITH Trinity Chapel, West End [W.80]
Z 1783-1837, B 1784-1837 [Mfc]

HARROW ON THE HILL [W.99]
Z 1826-36 [Mfc]

NORFOLK

DISS (Part Bapt)
Z 1806-36 [80]

FRAMLINGHAM PIGOT (Part Bapt)
Z 1808-36 [80]

SAXLINGHAM THORPE (Part Bapt)
ZR 1793-1837 [80]

SHELFANGER
Z 1795-1837 [80]

NORTHAMPTONSHIRE

KETTERING Gold Street
CB Extr 1785-1837 [39]

RINGSTEAD (Part Bapt)
Z 1811-36 [25]

THRAPSTON
Z 1794-1836, A 1795-1807,
B 1794-1837 [25]

WELLINGBOROUGH
ZC 1795-1837, DB 1792-1836 [25]

NORTHUMBERLAND

HEXHAM
C 1651-80 [32]

NOTTINGHAMSHIRE

NOTTINGHAM
Friar Lane & George Street
ZB 1742-1837 [L9];
Paradise Place Z 1806-37 [83]

OXFORDSHIRE

CHIPPING NORTON
Z(I) 1767-1831, Z 1767-1837,
B(I) 1788-1940 [P]

CO(A)TE BAMPTON
Z 1647-1837, M 1775-1839,
B 1647-1882

HOOK NORTON
Z 1772-1837, M 1844-77 B 1841-56

SYDENHAM
Z 1821-37

THAME
Z 1826-36, D 1828-36

SHROPSHIRE

BRIDGNORTH Castle Street
ZB 1779-1836 [1]

BROSELEY Birch Meadow
Z(I) 1835-37, Z 1794-1835 [1,104]

CHIRBURY (Part Bapt)
Z 1829-35 [104]

PONTESBURY
AD 1828-36 [104]

SHIFNAL
Z 1811-36 [104]

SHREWSBURY Claremont
Z 1766-1837 [1,104,112]

SOMERSETSHIRE

FROME Badcox Lane
A 1834-1961 [Mf]

STAFFORDSHIRE

COSELEY
Coppice Part Bapt) Z 1794-1837;
(Providence Bapt) ZR 1809-37;
Darkhouse Z 1822-37 [128]

WOLVERHAMPTON Walsall Street
(Bapt)
Z 1832-37 [127]

SUFFOLK

BARDWELL (Part Bapt)
Z 1817, 1820-37 [257]

CLARE
D or B 1822-37 [263]

SURREY

BETCHWORTH Brockham
Z 1781-1837 [21, Mfc]

CHOBHAM, West End Chapel
Z 1810-36, DB 1824 [21, Mfc]

CLAPHAM [W.76]
Z 1781-1836 [21, Mfc]

KINGSTON-UPON-THAMES [W78]
Z 1781-1837, D 1799-1836,
B 1799-1837 [21, Mfc]

SOUTHWARK, Christchurch [W.72]
Z 1772-1827 [Mf]

WANDSWORTH, Bridge Field [W122]
Z 1816-37, B 1825-36 [21, Mfc]

SUSSEX

BILLINGSHURST (Gen Bapt/Free
Christ Ch.(Unitarian))
D 1755-1980 [175]

BODLE STREET near Warbleton
ADB 1863-1901 [P]

BRIGHTON Bond Street (Salem Part
Bapt)
Z 1775-1837, B 1783-1834 [23]

DITCHLING (Gen Bapt)
ZR 1813-33, DB 1821-1836,
B 1837-1901 [64/5]

HAILSHAM
ZR 1795-1837 [23]

HORSHAM (Gen Bapt)
Z 1628-1836, DB 1720-69,
1771-1837 [23]

LEWES (Part Bapt)
Z 1775-1836 [23]

ROTHERFIELD
Z 1748-1836 [23]

RYE (Part Bapt)
Z 1769-1836, DB 1768-1837 [23]

UCKFIELD Rockhall
Z 1783-1836 [23]

WADHURST (Part Bapt)
Z 1812-37, B 1832-36 [23]

WIVELSFIELD (Part Bapt)
Z 1771-1836, B 1785-92 [22, 65]

WARWICKSHIRE

SHIPSTON-ON-STOUR
Z 1783-1836

WESTMORLAND

KENDAL (Unit Bapt)
Z 1801-39 [L4]

WILTSHIRE

DEVIZES (New Baptist)
AD 1805-1945

WORCESTERSHIRE

BROMSGROVE (Ind & Bapt)
C 1788-96, 1803-36;
Catshill A 1830-37

CRADLEY
Z 1794-1837, DB 1801-37 [15]

DUDLEY
Z 1816-37, D 1814-37 [19]

YORKSHIRE

BARNOLDSWICK Bridge Chapel
Z 1785-1837, B 1785-1817 [180, Mfc]

EARBY
Z 1802-37 [180]

SALTERFORTH
ZR 1753-1837, B 1756-1837 [Mfc]

WALES

BRECKNOCKSHIRE

MAESYBERLLAN (Part Bapt)
Z 1803-37 [68]

DENBIGHSHIRE

LLANFWROG
ZR 1790-1837 [77]

LLANNEFYDD
Z 1805-37 [78]

LLANSANNAN
Z 1814-30 [78]

GLAMORGAN

CARDIFF Bethany
Z 1804-37, D 1807-37 [8]

RADNORSHIRE

LLANANNO
Z 1792-1837 [37]

MAESYRHELEM *see* Llananno

OVERSEAS

AUSTRALIA

HOBART, Tasmania
B 1835-86

CANADA

QUEBEC (Area)
ZMB 1858-82 [Mf]

INDIA

CALCUTTA (Lall-Bazar)
A 1800-1908 [IND/L19]

UNITED STATES

NEW JERSEY

BETHLEHEM, HUNTERDON
COUNTY
M 1831-68 [P]

CAPE MAY
M 1808-22 [P]

KINGWOOD, HUNTERDON
COUNTY
M 1831-68 [P]

MIDDLETOWN
A 1721-87, D 1786-1811 [US/NY/G12]

NEW HAMPTON, HUNTERDON
COUNTY
M 1831-68 [P]

PITTSGROVE (DARETOWN),
SALEM COUNTY
M 1772-93 [P]

WASHINGTON TOWNSHIP
(Hamilton Sq.), MERCER COUNTY
M 1837-54 [P]

PENNSYLVANIA

PHILADELPHIA (1st Bapt)
M 1761-1803 [2]

NOTES

82

APPENDIX 3

A LIST OF THE ENGLISH BAPTIST CHURCH RECORDS
IN THE CUSTODY OF THE
GOSPEL STANDARD BAPTIST LIBRARY
5 HOVE PARK GARDENS,
HOVE, EAST SUSSEX BN3 6HN

Abbreviations: (P)=Photocopy; (Ts)=Transcript

NOTE: The W numbers in square brackets relate to the number allocated to the church in Whitley, W T, *The Baptists of London* (London 1928)

BERKSHIRE

FARINGDON   Church Book   1872-91

CAMBRIDGESHIRE

GODMANCHESTER *see* **HUNTINGDONSHIRE**

KIRTLING   Church Book[1]
                       List of Members[1]   1893-1904

ESSEX

BURNHAM-ON-CROUCH   Church Book   1861-1905

WITHAM   Church Book   1830-41
                       Church Book   1884-1975
                       Register of Members   1884

---

1. Now deposited with County Record Office, Shire Hall, Cambridge CB3 0AP.

GLOUCESTERSHIRE

TETBURY	Church Book	1858-1909

HAMPSHIRE

BARTLEY Hope Chapel, Totton Road	Church Book	1872-1960
LONGPARISH	Church Book	1818-1914

HERTFORDSHIRE

HERTFORD Ebenezer Chapel	Church Books[2]	1773-1928

HUNTINGDONSHIRE

GODMANCHESTER	Register of Births[3] Church Books[3]	1801-36 1825-1947

KENT

CANTERBURY Zoar Chapel, Burgate Lane	Church Books	1843-1913
RAINHAM Providence Chapel, Orchard Street	Church Book	1895-1914
TENTERDEN Jireh Chapel	Church Books	1844-1950

---

2. Now deposited with County Record Office, Hertford SG13 8DE.
3. Now deposited with County Record Office, Grammar School Walk, Huntingdon, Cambs PE18 6LF.

LANCASHIRE

BOLTON
Dorset Street, Church Books   1876-1956
formerly King Street

LEICESTERSHIRE

DESFORD   Church Book   1795-1809

OAKHAM: *see* **RUTLANDSHIRE**

LONDON

CHELSEA
Grove Chapel [W.192] Church Book   1850-99
Drayton Gardens, Church Books   1914-43
West Brompton, SW10

FOREST HILL
Zion Chapel [W.576] Church Book   1907-63
Malham Road, SE23

HAMPSTEAD
Ebenezer Chapel Church Books   1825-1957
[W.133] Christchurch
Passage, New End, NW3

WHITECHAPEL
Zoar Chapel [W.92] Church Records from 1808
Great Alie Street, E1 Church Book   1845-79
         Church Book   1881-1970

OXFORDSHIRE

FARINGDON: *see* **BERKSHIRE**

RUTLANDSHIRE

OAKHAM

Providence Chapel,	Church Book	1843-93
New Street	Church Book	1895-1954

SUFFOLK

LOWESTOFT

Tonning Street	Church Book	1868-1916

SURREY

DORKING

Holmwood Chapel	Church Book (Ts)	1885-1906
	Church Book	1907-36

LINGFIELD

Salem Chapel	Church Book	1925-75

SUSSEX

PELL GREEN	Church Book[4]	1820-44
SHOVERS GREEN	Church Books[4]	1816-61
	Church Book[4]	1865-1977

WILTSHIRE

AVEBURY	Church Book (P)[5]	1830-73
	Church Book (P)[5]	1892-1928
CORSHAM	Church Book (P)[5]	1858-1977

---

4. Now deposited with East Sussex County Archivist, The Maltings, Castle Precincts, Lewes, East Sussex BN7 1YT.
5. The originals of these registers are now deposited with Wiltshire County Record Office, County Hall, Trowbridge, Wiltshire BA14 8JG.

LUDGERSHALL	Church Book (P)[6]	1818-19
MARKET LAVINGTON	Church Book (P)[6]	1832-1932
UPAVON	Church Books (P)[6]	1858-1978

---

6. The originals of these registers are now deposited with Wiltshire County Record Office, County Hall, Trowbridge, Wiltshire BA14 8JG.

NOTES

APPENDIX 4

A LIST OF THE ENGLISH BAPTIST CHURCH RECORDS IN THE CUSTODY OF THE STRICT BAPTIST HISTORICAL SOCIETY'S LIBRARY, DUNSTABLE BAPTIST CHAPEL, ST MARY'S GATE, DUNSTABLE, BEDFORDSHIRE LU6 3SW

Abbreviations: (P) = Photocopy; (Ts) = Transcript

NOTE: The W numbers in square brackets relate to the number allocated to the church in Whitley, W T, *The Baptists of London* (London 1928)

BEDFORDSHIRE

RISELY (now RISELEY)	Church Minutes	1839-1952
SHARNBROOK Bethlehem Chapel	Church Minutes	1833-1904

BERKSHIRE

MAIDENHEAD Providence Chapel	Church Minutes	1863-1913

BUCKINGHAMSHIRE

ASKETT	Church Minutes	1914-40
ICKFORD	Church Book (P)	1825-69
IVINGHOE	Register of Births	1793-1837
	Record of Baptisms	1804-13
	Church Book (P)	1804-1973
	(including Births	1793-1817
	and Burials	1890-91

LONG CRENDON	Church Book (P)	1845-57
	Membership Lists (P)	1845-61
PENN	Church Books	1828-1929
	Membership Lists	1802-93
	Membership Lists	1900-25
WADDESDON HILL	Church Book	1794-1836
	Church Book	1846-1974
	Register of Burials	1851-1974
WINSLOW	Church Book	1807-53
	Register of Births	1818-36
	Register of Deaths	1856-92
WOOBURN GREEN	Church Minutes	c.1849-63
	Church Minutes	1887-1916
	Standing Minutes	c.1919-39
	Church Minutes	1939-43
	Church Minutes	1966-79

CAMBRIDGESHIRE

BENWICK	Church Book	1858-
	Church Minutes	1908-11
	Church Minutes	1923
	Church Minutes	1937-63
	Marriages	1930, 1934, 1946
	List of Deaths	1860-1959
CAMBRIDGE	Church Minutes	1897-1976
Tenison Road	Membership Roll	1897-1955
COTTENHAM		
Ebenezer Chapel,	Church Minutes	1819-1979
Rooks Lane	Membership Lists	1861-1979
	Register of Births	1800-44

ELSWORTH	Church Minutes	1887-1953
STAPLEFORD		
Providence Chapel	Church Book	1851-66
	Church Book	1877-1926
	Membership Roll	1877-97
WILLINGHAM		
First Church	Church Book	1726-
	Church Minutes	1835-1926
	Register of Births	1792-1833
	Births	1790-1820
	Baptisms	1754-1826
	Marriages	1842-59
	Membership Lists	1749-1937

DEVONSHIRE

NEWTON ABBOT		
Old Baptist Chapel,	Church Book	1819-71
East Street	Church Book	1874-1919

ESSEX

EAST MERSEA	Church Minutes	1804-1902
HARWICH		
Ebenezer Chapel,	Church Minutes	1821-1944
King's Head Street		
(originally Hart Street)		
SAFFRON WALDEN	Church Minutes	1820-1938
London Road	Membership Roll	1820-1937

GLOUCESTERSHIRE

CIRENCESTER	Church Minutes	1879-1915
Park Street	Membership List	1840-1908

CUBBERLEY (now COBERLEY)

	Church Minutes	1835-1930
	Membership Roll	1827-1918

MARSHFIELD	Church Minutes	1854-1920
Ebenezer Chapel	Membership List	1854-1908

HERTFORDSHIRE

HERTFORD
Port Vale Independent   Church Book (P)   1835-67
Calvinistic Chapel

HITCHIN
Bethel Chapel   Church Book (P)   *c.*1850-61

HITCHIN	Church Minutes	1858-92
Providence Chapel	Membership List	1858-90

LONG MARSTON	Church Boook (P)	1862-1953
	Church Book (P)	1955-71
	Membership Roll, revised (P)	1932

HUNTINGDONSHIRE

HAIL WESTON	Church Book	1757-1866
	Church Book	1869-1901

ST NEOTS	Register of Births	1808-42
New Lane	Register of Burials	1853-96

KENT

BETHERSDEN	Church Book (Ts)	1809-1915
Union Chapel	Births (Ts)	1799-1836

BROADSTAIRS
Providence Chapel,
62a High Street

	Church Minutes	1878-1941

EGERTON

	Church Books (Ts)	1836-1915
	Membership List (Ts)	1836-1971
	Register of Burials (Ts)	1863-1984

HADLOW

	Church Minutes	1831-55
	Church Minutes	1858-1923

MAIDSTONE
Providence Chapel,
Mote Road

	Church Book	1852-1943

SMARDEN
Tilden Chapel

	Register of Marriages (Ts)	1840-1984
	Register of Burials (Ts)	1837-1984

TENTERDEN
Jireh Chapel

	Register of Burials (Ts)	1870-1983

LANCASHIRE

ACCRINGTON
Zion Chapel,
Blackburn Road

	Church Minutes (Ts)	1867-84
	Church Minutes	1888-1926
	Membership List	1867-88

PRESTON
Zoar Chapel

	Church Minutes	1852-79

ROSSENDALE
Ring's Row,
Crawshawbooth

	Church Book	1827-53

SABDEN

	Church Book	1835-43
	Membership List	1835-49

STREETGATE

'Zion's Hill',	Church Book	1852-82
Little Hulton,	Church Minutes	1879-80
Bolton	Membership List	1852-82

LINCOLNSHIRE

BILLINGBOROUGH

| High Bridge Street | Church Minutes | 1867-90 |

LONDON

ACTON

| Tabernacle [W.609], | Church Minutes | 1881-1971 |
| Acton Lane, W3 | | |

BETHNAL GREEN

| Shalom Chapel [W.307], | Church Minutes | 1889-1908 |
| 'Oval', Hackney Road, E2 | | |

| BRENTFORD | Church Book (P) | 1853-76 |

DEPTFORD

Zion Chapel [W.177],	Church Book	1842-81
New Cross Road, SE14	Membership List	1887-90
(originally in	Deacons' Minute Books	1875-1941
Giffin Street)	Deacons' Minute Books	1949-58

FULHAM

| Ebenezer Chapel [W.693], | Church Minutes | 1913-72 |
| Lillie Road, SW6 | Register of Members | 1889-1940 |

ISLINGTON

Zoar Chapel [W.258],	Church Minutes	1899-1958
Holloway, Tollington		
Park, N4		

ISLINGTON

Ebenezer Chapel [W.391],	Church Minutes	1875-98
Upper Holloway,	Church Minutes	1902-20
Elthorne Road,	Church Minutes	1935-46
Hornsey Rise, N19	Membership List	1905-40

LEWISHAM

Ladywell [W.832],	Church Book	1910-11
Whitburn Hall,		
Whitburn Road, SE13		

WESTMINSTER

Pimlico [W.129],	Church Minutes	1839-56
Carmel Chapel,		
Westbourne Street, SW1		

MIDDLESEX

BRENTFORD: *see* **LONDON**

NORFOLK

GREAT ELLINGHAM	Church Roll (P)	1701-89

NORWICH

Orford Hill	Church Minutes	1857-1975
	Membership Roll	1858-1911

SHELFANGER	Church Book	1758-1825
	Church Books	1834-1940
	Membership Lists	1765-1825
	Membership Lists	1834-77
	Membership Lists	1880-1920
	Register of Births	1758-1824
	Marriages	1904-20

NORTHAMPTONSHIRE

NORTHAMPTON
Providence Chapel,	Church Minutes	1835-1984
Abington Street.	Membership Lists	1810-1968
Removed to		
The Headlands, 1957		

OUNDLE
Zion Chapel,	Church Minutes	1846-95
Chapel End	Membership List	1800-95

NOTTINGHAMSHIRE

SUTTON-IN-ASHFIELD
Walstone Lane Chapel	Church Book (Ts)	1770-1865

SUFFOLK

BUNGAY
Bethesda Chapel,	Church Books	1852-1960
Chaucer Street	Membership List	c.1846-1939

BURY ST EDMUNDS
Rehoboth Chapel,	Church Minutes	1895-96
Westgate Street		

FRISTON
	Church Minutes	1879-1906

GLEMSFORD
Providence Chapel,	Church Minutes	1859-1911
Hunts Hill		

SURREY

CHOBHAM
West End	Church Book	1798-1806
	Church Book	1847-56
	Church Book	1858-86

CROYDON	Church Minutes	1901-70
Derby Road [W.540]	Deacons' Minutes	1920-79
	Membership Registers	1892-1974

HORLEY		
Providence Chapel,	Church Minutes	1846-1945
Lee Street (1846-92),	Membership List	1846-92
Victoria Road (1892-)		

KINGSTON-UPON-THAMES		
Zion Chapel [W.292],	Church Book	1922-59
Norbiton, London Road		

SUSSEX

| EAST GRINSTEAD | | |
| Providence | Church Book | 1890-1952 |

WILTSHIRE

NETHERAVON	Church Minutes (sparse)	1872-1948
	Membership List	1835-1913
	Baptismal List	1834-71

YORKSHIRE

| MASBOROUGH | Church Minutes | 1862-64 |
| | Church Minutes | 1874-1983 |